Teacher's Guide for Supplementary Materials
Second Edition
To accompany
PUNTOS DE PARTIDA
An Invitation to Spanish
Fifth Edition

Sharon Foerster
Jean Miller
University of Texas at Austin

The McGraw-Hill Companies, Inc.
Primis Custom Publishing

New York St. Louis San Francisco Auckland Bogotá
Caracas Lisbon London Madrid Mexico Milan Montreal
New Delhi Paris San Juan Singapore Sydney Tokyo Toronto

McGraw-Hill
A Division of The McGraw-Hill Companies

TEACHER'S GUIDE FOR SUPPLEMENTARY MATERIALS TO ACCOMPANY
PUNTOS DE PARTIDA: AN INVITATION TO SPANISH

McGraw-Hill's Primis Custom Publishing consists of products that are produced from camera-ready copy.
Peer review, class testing, and accuracy are primarily the responsibility of the author(s).

2 3 4 5 6 7 8 9 0 GDP GDP 9 0 9 8 7

ISBN 0-07-007605-7

Editor: Judy Wetherington
Printer/Binder: Greyden Press

TO THE TEACHER

Supplementary Materials to Accompany *Puntos de Partida* started as an attempt to give some extra help to the first-semester Spanish instructors at the University of Texas at Austin. We wanted to provide these teachers with materials that were correlated to the text, classroom-tested, easily accessible, and in line with the teaching philosophy of the department.

We have been gratified at the success of the first and subsequent editions of the *Supplement*, and are pleased to bring you this new edition, intended to be used with the fifth edition of *Puntos de Partida*.

What will you find in the new *Supplementary Materials* and the accompanying *Teacher's Guide*?

- Communicative Goals and Grammatical Structures checklists – Each chapter of the *Supplement* and *Teacher's Guide* opens with a list of communicative goals and grammatical structures covered in that chapter. These checklists are a quick, concise reminder to students of what they will be focusing on in a particular chapter.

- Pronunciation – Extra pronunciation practice, ranging from tongue-twisters to proverbs to word-association games.

- Listening comprehension – For each chapter, we provide a wide variety of listening-comprehension activities, including picture descriptions, chart completions, and lists of chapter-related questions, definitions, and true-false statements. In the *Teacher's Guide* you will find all the listening scripts.

- Grammar – You will find many classroom tested grammar practices, such as cloze passages, sentence completion worksheets, charts, picture descriptions and more. New to this edition of the *Supplement* are many art-based grammar practices, as well as worksheets that have been contextualized for each chapter. The clear explanations accompanying each practice allow students to work on them outside of class. They may also be used as quiz or test material, extra credit, and review. Answers to many of these exercises are included at the end of the *Teacher's Guide*.

- Chapter Review – For each chapter, we provide comprehensive yet concise reviews. These reviews target vocabulary, grammar, and communicative goals, and are ideal for test preparation.

- Integrative Activities – We offer a variety of creative, communicative activities combining the four skills, each designed to get students moving, thinking, and talking in Spanish.

- Guided Writings – Fun, art-based writing assignments focusing on current and previous chapter vocabulary and structures. In the *Teacher's Guide* you will find suggestions for follow-up activities.

- Communicative Goals Practices – New to this edition of the *Supplement* are five art-based speaking activities designed to get students to practice and review the communicative tasks they have been learning. Each practice features a picture for students to describe and list of targeted goals for them to incorporate in their descriptions. These practices are excellent for preparation for oral interviews.

- Games – Finally, for each chapter we provide suggestions for classroom-tested games, from Password to chapter-related Bingos to verb relay races, with instructions on how to set them up.

The *Supplementary Materials* and *Teacher's Guide* are meant, first and last, to be a time-saver when doing lesson plans. Here, in one manual, you will find a wide range of imaginative, tested materials and activities, designed by experienced teachers who have taught extensively with *Puntos*. It is our earnest hope that this manual and Guide will make your lives easier when planning classes, and that you and your students find the materials interesting, enjoyable, and beneficial.

Dr. Sharon Foerster
Jean Miller
University of Texas at Austin
June, 1997

ANTE TODO

Communicative Goals for Ante Todo
By the end of the chapter students should be able to:

* meet and greet others ☐
* describe themselves and others ☐
* count to 30 and do simple math ☐
* talk about likes and dislikes ☐
* tell time ☐
* get information by asking questions ☐

Grammatical Structures
Students should know:

* **ser** ☐
* interrogative words ☐
* **gustar** ☐
* **hay** ☐

I. PRONUNCIATION

A. Short poems. This first poem, and 12 sentences filled with cognates and lots of vowels, are on p. 1 of the Student Supplement. Have students memorize the first poem so you can always refer back to it if students mispronounce their vowels. The second poem can be enlarged and put on a transparency for more practice.

A E I O U
Arbolito de Perú
¿Cómo te llamas tú?

Ronda del zapatero

Tipi tape, tipi tape
tipi tape, tipitón
tipi tape; zapa zapa
zapatero remendón.

Tipi tape todo el día,
todo el día tipitón;
tipi tape, macha macha,
machacando en tu rincón.

Tipi tape en tu banquete,
tipi tape, tipitón;
tipitón con tu martillo,
macha macha, machacón.

B. Spelling Practice. Have students stand up with a notebook in hand and circulate around the classroom asking 5 students their names in Spanish. They must copy the names as they are spelled to them

— ¿Cómo te llamas?
— Me llamo Juan Headley.
— ¿Cómo?
— Juan Headley. J–U–A–N H–E–A–D–L–E–Y.

C. Pronunciation and Geography Practice. (Student Supplement, p. 2) This exercise offers another opportunity for students to practice their Spanish vowels. You should read aloud and have students repeat chorally. Student especially enjoy repeating the longer sentences.

D. List of cognates. (Student Supplement, p. 3) Students can work in pairs to come up with ten combinations from the three lists of nouns and one list of adjectives. Five of the combinations should be logical and five should be funny "combinaciones locas." Circulate and correct them as need be.

II. LISTENING COMPREHENSION

A. Cierto/Falso. Make up true/false statements using cognates. Below are some samples. Read the following instructions to the students: "You will hear a series of statements in Spanish. Write C (**cierto**) if the statement is true and F (**falso**) if the statement is false. You will hear each sentence twice."

1. El elefante es un animal enorme.
2. Canadá es un país tropical.
3. El Atlántico es una isla caribeña.
4. La televisión es una invención moderna.
5. Ronald Reagan fue el presidente de Francia.
6. El mosquito es una fruta tropical.
7. El teléfono es un instrumento de tortura.
8. Nueva York es la capital de California.
9. Colin Powell es un general chino.
10. Benjamín Franklin es un indio de Sudamérica.

B. Preguntas personales. By the end of each chapter, students should be able to respond orally to and ask each other a series of questions. These questions are good as warm-up exercises. You can ask students the questions or call on them to ask each other "Pregúntale a Marta, '¿Cómo está?'" They ask the questions using the **tú** form.

These are the questions students should be able to respond to by the end of **Ante Todo**:

1. ¿Cómo te llamas?
2. ¿Cómo se llama él/ella?
3. ¿Cómo estás?
4. ¿Cómo eres tú?
5. ¿Cómo es (*person's name*)?
6. ¿Qué hora es?
7. ¿Cuántas personas hay en la clase/en la foto?
8. ¿Cuál es la capital de Texas/de Costa Rica?
9. ¿A qué hora es la clase de español?
10. ¿Cuánto es el libro de español?
11. ¿Dónde está San Francisco/Barcelona/Bogotá?
12. ¿Cómo se llama el presidente/el profesor de español?
13. ¿Te gusta la música moderna/la clase de español?
14. ¿Te gustan las enchiladas?
15. ¿Cómo se llama tu actor favorito? ¿Tu novela favorita?

III. GRAMMAR

A. La hora y los saludos. (Student Supplement, p. 4) Practices greeting and telling time.

B. Preguntas y respuestas. (Student Supplement, p. 5) This two-part worksheet practices interrogative words and question formation.

IV. INTEGRATIVE ACTIVITIES

A. Descripciones de personas famosas--¿Quién soy? First, distribute a list of famous people to each student in the class (see partial list of suggestions below). Then give each student an additional slip of paper with the name of one famous person on it. When everyone has a paper (tell them not to reveal the names), give the students 2-3 minutes to write a description to the celebrity without naming the person. They may refer to the adjective list on pp. 6-7 of *Puntos* and incorporate any other adjectives you choose to introduce. Each student then reads, in turn, his or her description; the rest of the class consults the list and guesses who is being described. Here is a partial list:

políticos	actores/actrices	músicos/cantantes/ escritores/pintores
Bill Clinton	Edward James Olmos	Sting
Boris Yeltsin	Michael Douglas	Gloria Estefan
Saddam Hussein	Brad Pitt	Madonna
Fidel Castro	David Letterman	Ernest Hemingway
Dan Quayle	Julia Roberts	Gabriel García Márquez
Henry Cisneros	Tom Cruise	Salvador Dalí
	Geraldo Rivera	Pablo Picasso
	Barbara Walters	Georgia O'Keefe
	Sharon Stone	Garth Brooks
	Andy García	Selena
		Courtney Love

Ejemplo: Soy actor. Soy cubano. Soy emocional y valiente. ¿Quién soy?
Respuesta: Andy García.

B. Adjective and Description Practice. An oral group activity. Solicit adjectives from students as a group to describe familiar things/places such as the following:

la clase de español
la comida de McDonald's
la universidad
el libro *Puntos de Partida*
la librería
el profesor/la profesora de español

You ask the students, for example, "¿Cómo es la clase de español?" You hear various responses offered by different students: "horrible," "interesante," "difícil," "fantástica," etc. You then combine these adjectives in one or two sentences, and then go on to the next item. This is a good way for students to become familiar with adjectival agreement, hearing you say "La clase es fantástica," etc.

IV. GAMES

A. "Hangman." Begin the game by thinking of a familiar word in Spanish and writing the number of blanks which correspond to the number of letters in the word on the board.

EXAMPLE: the word you think of is "presidente," so on the board you put 9 blanks.

The class then guesses letters which fill in the blanks; they must use Spanish pronunciation and guess correctly. After students do a couple of words with you, you may want to have a few of them come up to the board with words of their own.

B. "Los números." Divide the class into pairs. Each person in the pair thinks of a number between 0-30, but doesn't tell his/her partner. The partner must guess the number in this way:

STUDENT 1: ¿Es 15?
STUDENT 2: No, es más de 15/es menos de 15.
STUDENT 1: ¿Es 8? etc.

You may want to model by having them guess, as a group, one or two of your numbers beforehand; also, you will have to introduce "más de/menos de" before the game.

CAPÍTULO 1

Communicative Goals for Chapter 1
By the end of the chapter students should be able to:

* talk about their college or university	☐
* discuss their class schedule, courses and professors	☐
* talk about activities they do on campus	☐
* get information by asking questions	☐

Grammatical Structures
Students should know:

* articles	☐
* **-ar** verbs	☐
* **estar**	☐
* negation	☐

I. PRONUNCIATION

A. For each chapter, pick 10-15 key words and practice them in a pronunciation drill. this kind of activity is good at the very start of a class. Tell students that they will remember vocabulary items better and longer if they use visualization and association techniques. In other words, they should picture a pencil when they learn the word **lápiz**, not the word *pencil.*

matrícula	consejera	mochila	extranjero	lápiz
bolígrafo	hombre	diccionario	escritorio	teléfono
edificio	residencia	librería	calculadora	apartamento

B. You may also see the pronunciation practice on p. 7 of the Supplement. These *dichos* offer good practice with the vowels.

II. LISTENING COMPREHENSION

A. Cierto/Falso. Make up some true/false or multiple choice statements using cognates. You already have some from Ante Todo; here are some more for Chapter 1. Tell your students to write **cierto** if the statement is true and **falso** if it is false. Verify comprehension in a follow-up.

1. (*Hold up your pen.*) Esta cosa es un lápiz.
2. Una residencia es un lugar para profesores.
3. Una librería es un lugar para estudiar.
4. Un consejero es una persona.
5. En la clase de español hay 10 personas.
6. En la clase hay una pizarra.
7. Una biblioteca es un edificio.
8. No hay sillas en la oficina del presidente de la universidad.
9. Hay muchos libros en la biblioteca.
10. La química, la biología y la fisica son ciencias.

Try these statements with cognates another day:

1. El rifle es un instrumento musical muy popular.
2. El tigre es un animal enorme en comparación con el elefante.

3. Hay varios tipos de cáncer que son fatales.
4. Una sinfonía es una composición musical para orquesta.
5. El chocolate es una forma de gas invisible.

B. Numbers Listening Exercise. Dictate sentences such as the following to your students. Tell them to pay careful attention to the number. The only thing they need to write down is the number. Verify comprehension afterwards.

1. El autobús número 12 va al parque.
2. El tren para Barcelona sale a las nueve menos cuarto.
3. Sólo tengo treinta pesetas. ¿Cuánto cuesta un lápiz?
4. Necesito tres clases más de español.
5. Mis cuadernos, bolígrafos y lápices cuestan $13.00 en total.
6. Hay fiestas importantes el 5 de mayo y el 16 de septiembre.

C. Listening Passages. Read the following passages slowly twice to your class while they complete the listening comprehension checks on p. 8 of the Student Supplement. Then have them respond to the **cierto/falso** comprehension questions afterwards.

1. You will hear a short passage about two friends followed by a series of true/false statements. Listen carefully.

   Roberto y Luis son amigos que trabajan en la Universidad de California. Roberto enseña biología y ciencias naturales; Luis no enseña porque es estudiante. Estudia historia y lenguas -- habla francés, alemán y español. Luis también trabaja. Trabaja en la librería porque necesita dinero para pagar la matrícula y comprar libros. Los dos amigos están muy contentos en la Universidad de California porque sus clases son buenas.

   CIERTO/FALSO
   1. Los dos amigos son estudiantes.
   2. Uno de los amigos habla muchas lenguas.
   3. Luis no trabaja porque es estudiante.
   4. Están contentos en la universidad porque las librerías son buenas.

   PREGUNTAS. Answer with short sentences.
   1. ¿Cómo se llaman los dos amigos?
   2. ¿Estudian los dos?
   3. ¿Dónde trabaja Luis?
   4. ¿Qué enseña Roberto?
   5. ¿Por qué trabaja Luis?

2. You will hear a short passage about two students followed by a series of true/false statements. Listen carefully.

   Ramón y María son dos estudiantes españoles. Son de Madrid, pero ahora están en la Argentina donde toman clases en la Universidad de Buenos Aires. Toman clases por la mañana, pero por la tarde muchas veces pasean (caminan) por la calle Florida. Allí ven a muchos de sus amigos y miran las muchas tiendas interesantes que hay. Como son estudiantes, son pobres y no pueden comprar mucho, ¡pero sí miran!

CIERTO/FALSO

1. Ramón y María son estudiantes.
2. Estudian en Buenos Aires.
3. Son de la Argentina.
4. Estudian por la mañana.
5. Caminan por la calle Florida con frecuencia.
6. Allí compran muchas cosas interesantes.

D. El horario del profesor/de la profesora. Distribute a chart to the students which looks something like the chart on p. 8 of the Teacher's Guide, but with only one block of space per hour. Then read aloud a schedule of your day to the class. (You may have to simplify things, since at this point the students only know **-ar** verbs.) As you speak, students listen and fill in the chart with the information. Deliberately leave some gaps open in your schedule and/or jump around a little. After reading the passage, check comprehension with oral questions such as: "¿Qué clase tomo a las dos?" ¿Qué cosa necesito tomar por la mañana?" etc.

Here is a sample **horario**:
Yo llego a la Universidad a las diez de la mañana. Primero, necesito tomar un café. Luego, voy a mi oficina y preparo unas actividades para las clases de español. Enseño la clase a las once en punto. Después, me gusta nadar en la piscina de la Universidad. Regreso al Departamento de Español porque tengo/tomo una clase de literatura a las dos. La clase es buena, ¡pero a veces estoy cansada y deseo tomar una siesta! Después de mi clase, hablo con mis amigos. Juntos, nosotros tomamos un café en la cafetería. Después yo voy a la biblioteca para buscar unos libros. Estudio en la biblioteca por dos horas. Finalmente, a las seis y media tomo el autobús de la Universidad y regreso a mi apartamento. A las siete veo televisión y después necesito estudiar.

E. Preguntas personales. It's a good idea to begin class with a few questions to get the students in a Spanish-speaking mood. Here are some possibilities for Chapter 1. Some teachers have found it convenient to keep these all on an index card and them simply refer to it each day. (You will probably find yourself tailoring these types of questions to the personality of your class.)

1. ¿Hablas francés?
2. ¿Hablamos español en clase?
3. ¿Estudias mucho?
4. ¿Trabajas? ¿Dónde?
5. ¿Cuándo estudias?
6. ¿A qué hora regresas a casa?
7. ¿Te gusta tomar café por la mañana?
8. ¿Te gusta bailar?
9. ¿Bailas bien?

10. ¿Buscas un apartamento?
11. ¿Qué necesitan Uds. para la clase de español?
12. ¿Dónde compras los libros?
13. ¿Cuántos deportes practicas?
14. ¿Quién paga la matrícula para ti?
15. ¿Dónde está el laboratorio de computadoras?
16. ¿Cuántas materias estudias este semestre? ¿Cuál es tu favorita?
17. ¿Quién enseña la clase?
18. ¿Quién canta bien en tu opinión?
19. ¿Cuántos exámenas deseas tomar este semestre?

III. GRAMMAR.

The following worksheets, included in the Student Supplement, can be used as homework assignments or classroom activities.

A. Los artículos definidos e indefinidos. (p. 9) Contrasts the meanings and uses of definite and indefinite articles.

B. Present tense of -AR verbs. (p. 10) This fill-in-the-blank worksheet covers the new Chapter 1 verbs.

C. Formas plurales. (p. 11) Contrasts singular and plural forms.

D. Preguntas y respuestas. (p. 12) This worksheet practices question formation and the new question words.

E. Repaso of Ante Todo and Chapter 1. You may want to assign this 5-page review a few days before the first test and include it in your test review activities. (pp. 12-17)

IV. INTEGRATIVE ACTIVITIES

Use these integrative activities toward the end of the chapter when students have more control over vocabulary and grammar structures.

A. El horario de la clase. This is a good group activity. First, on the board draw a big chart which looks something like this:

	Estudiante 1	Estudiante 2	Estudiante 3	Estudiante 4
9:00				
10:00				
11:00				
12:00				
1:00				

You can change the hours to the left of the chart to fit closer to the time(s) you teach. Then select four students and begin to ask them questions about their daily schedule: "¿Tomas una clase a las nueve?", "¿Qué clase es", ¿Cómo es el profesor?", "¿Dónde es la clase?", etc. Fill in the chart with appropriate information as you go along. Involve the other students in the class by asking them to compare their schedules with those on the board. Example: "Jorge, ¿tomas una clase a las 9:00 también?", "¿Qué clase es?", "¿Te gusta?", etc. The questions you can ask your students in this activity are practically endless. As a follow-up, you might ask each student to write out his or her daily schedule in Spanish for homework.

B. ¿Qué clases tomas este semestre? (Student Supplement, p. 18) Have students fill out the first chart with their own schedules. Then have them find a partner to fill out the second chart. Model questions are on the activity sheet. At the end of this activity, each pair of students needs to see if there is an hour during the week when they can get together to have a coffee.

C. Situations and Dialogues. Towards the end of Chapter 1, set aside time for student-created dialogues. This is a good integrative activity. Tell students to divide up into groups of 2 or 3, and tell them to pick one of the three following situations and develop it into a dialogue. Give them five minutes to get themselves organized and write out a mini-script (make sure they know the time limit). Then, have the students present their dialogues to the rest of the class. As a follow-up, spend a few moments after all the presentations correcting common errors.

Here are the three possible situations. If you choose to use this activity for dialogue practice, you can make copies of these situations for each of your students.

DIÁLOGOS

1. You are a Latin-American student taking a tour of the university. Ask your tour guide some questions: what s/he studies, how the classes are, if s/he lives in a dorm, if the university is expensive, etc.
2. You have just met an interesting person in the cafeteria of the Universidad de Granada. Strike up a conversation asking: if s/he is a student at the University, what s/he studies, if s/he works and where, if s/he wants to have coffee late (**más tarde**), etc.
3. Imagine you are a clerk in the bookstore and a Costa Rican student needs some help. Approach the student and ask: what books s/he needs; if s/he wants to buy paper, pencils, or notebooks; if s/he wants to pay for the books in cash (**al contado**), etc. You can say that you will look for the items the customer needs and thank him or her.

V. GAMES. Here are three games that are great for practicing vocabulary and **gustar**.

A. Gustar Bingo. (Student Supplement, p. 19) Before beginning the game, do some preliminary work with **te gusta, me gusta, no me gusta**, etc. Introduce the use of **me gustan** and **te gustan** for plural subjects. Do this activity once the students have these constructions down. Tell students that they may only ask ONE question of each student; when they receive a "Sí, me gusta(n)" as a response, they write down that person's name in the bingo square. If they receive a "No, no me gusta(n)" as a response, then they must move on to someone else.

At the end of the game have the winner(s) report on their findings. This is a perfect opportunity to introduce "Le gusta(n)" when talking about a third party. For example, the winning student will tell the class: "A Bubba le gusta Jerry Seinfeld." If you have time and the students are still interested, you can use this game to lead into informal practice with **gustar**. Find out how many people like Chinese food, how many don't like dancing, and so forth.

B. Password. Write down the vocabulary words from the list at the end of Chapter 1 on slips of paper. Distribute one or two slips to each student, telling him/her not to let anyone else see. Divide the class into two teams. Then instruct one member of Team A to define a word to another member of Team A; if the second student guesses correctly, then their team wins a point. If not, Team B has the chance to try, and so on. It's very useful to model two or three definitions for your students before the game. Tell them to begin their instructions using the cognate category words from **Ante Todo: es un lugar, es una cosa, es una persona, es una comida, es un animal**, etc.

EXAMPLE: Es una cosa. Es una cosa para los libros. Es una cosa que usamos para llevar los libros.
ANSWER: mochila

C. Pictionary. This is a vocabulary-based game similar in structure to PASSWORD. Again, write down words from Chapter 1 (pick some abstract words that are difficult to draw) and divide the class into two groups. Each group selects one member to go to the chalkboard. You show the first word to those two students, but not to anyone else. the two students, using separate chalkboards, attempt to draw the word given them while their respective teams guess. The two teams may NOT look at each other's chalkboards, but can LISTEN to clues being offered by the members of the opposing team. The team that correctly guesses the word first wins a point (keep them to a time limit). After one word has been guessed, two new members are chosen to draw.

CAPÍTULO 2

Communicative Goals for Chapter 2
By the end of the chapter students should be able to:

* talk about family relationships	☐
* identify a person's nationality	☐
* tell your age and birthday	☐
* indicate purpose and reason for doing something	☐
* introduce people	☐

Grammatical Structures
Students should know:

* **ser**	☐
* **-er** and **-ir** verbs	☐
* placement of adjectives	☐

I. PRONUNCIATION

A. It is a good idea to do a group pronunciation warm-up at the beginning of class. On p. 65 of *Puntos*, Exercises A and B have lists of words with which to practice. Do this with the books open so that the students can see the words as they pronounce them.

B. At this stage students really enjoy practicing sentences with lots of the same sounds. Try these on p. 21 of the Student Supplement. After you model the sentences and have the class repeat them chorally, have students work in pairs to practice more.

1. Tu tía Tula tiene treinta tortillas tostadas.
2. Mi padre y mi primo, Paquito, practican con su profesor, Pablo Pérez.
3. Imelda es impaciente, incompetente e indiscreta.
4. Patricia Pineda es práctica, patriótica y poética.
5. Lola López Ludwig, la alemana, está en Lima hasta el lunes.
6. En general Geraldo Germán es religioso y generoso.

II. LISTENING COMPREHENSION

A. Cierto/Falso. Continue testing the students' understanding by giving them true/false or multiple-choice statements. You may do this type of exercise as a practice or a pop quiz; in either case, verify comprehension afterwards. Here are some sample statements:

1. El hijo de mi hermano es mi nieto.
2. Roma es una ciudad italiana.
3. El alcohol es un líquido, el oxígeno es un gas y el metal es un sólido.
4. Los astronautas norteamericanos van al espacio en motocicleta.
5. La hija de mi tía es mi prima.
6. El bolígrafo de la profesora es de plástico.
7. El rifle, el torpedo y el cañón son armas.
8. Las personas antipáticas tienen muchos amigos.
9. *Anna Karenina* es una novela larga, y Magic Johnson es un hombre alto.
10. Los alumnos trabajadores estudian; los alumnos perezosos toman siestas.

Multiple Choice

1. La guitarra es: a) un instrumento musical, b) una máquina electrónica, c) un animal exótico.
2. Yo soy el hijo de Roberto y Alicia. Roberto y Alicia son: a) mis parientes, b) mis padres, c) mis tíos.
3. El padre de mi padre es mi: a) primo, b) abuelo, c) tío.
4. Michael Jordan es un jugador de baloncesto muy bueno, tiene mucho talento y, naturalmente, es muy: a) largo, b) alto, c) mayor.
5. Mi hermano Miguel está casado. Su esposa se llama Paquita. Paquita es mi: a) nieta, b) cuñada, c) sobrina.
6. Yo tengo 19 dólares en mi mochila; mi amigo Diego tiene 40 dólares. ¿Cuánto dinero tenemos en total? a) $29, b) $49, c) $59.
7. Yo tengo casi 25 años y mi hermano Roberto tiene 27. Por eso, Roberto es mi hermano: a) mayor, b) menor, c) viejo.
8. Mi tía Susana está casada con un hombre que se llama Ernesto. Susana y Ernesto tienen 4 hijos. Los hijos de ellos son mis: a) nietos, b) primos, c) hermanos.

B. Preguntas personales. These are good warm-up questions. You can also photocopy these questions and have students walk around the class asking 5 different classmates 2 questions each. This can be done a few times a week. It helps them to get to know each other and to practice real communication.

1. ¿Es grande o pequeña tu familia?
2. ¿Cuántos hermanos tienes?
3. ¿Cuántos años tienen?
4. ¿Cómo se llaman tus hermanos?
5. ¿Quién es tu primo favorito? ¿Por qué?
6. ¿De dónde son tus abuelos paternales?
7. ¿Dónde viven tus padres?
8. ¿Cuándo comes en la casa de tus padres?
9. ¿Te gusta vivir en la casa de tus padres?
10. ¿Cuándo regresas a la casa de tus padres?
11. ¿De quién es la mochila? ¿el cuaderno? ¿el sombrero?
12. ¿Quién en la clase es alto? ¿moreno? ¿rubia? ¿trabajador?
13. ¿Eres perezoso?
14. ¿Quién tiene un perro? ¿Cómo se llama? ¿Cómo es?
15. ¿Comes y miras televisión al mismo tiempo?
16. ¿Por qué debes asistir a clase todos los días?
17. ¿A qué hora llegas a la clase de español normalmente?
18. ¿Cuántas horas estudias español cada día?
19. ¿Quién comprende tus problemas?
20. ¿A qué hora abre la biblioteca?

C. Dictado. Another idea for listening comprehension is practice with numbers. Here is a possibility for dictating telephone numbers. (Verify comprehension afterwards by having 5 students write their answers on the board. Ask the class if the answers are correct.)

1. El número de Concha es el 9-23-57-98.
2. El número de mi abuela es el 6-54-69-11.
3. El número de la profesora es el 8-82-18-07.
4. El número de Carmencita es el 5-45-76-15.
5. El número de Rafael es el 7-08-33-14.

D. Listening Passages. Read the following passages to the students twice. Then ask them to respond to the following questions (which are short and easy enough to just read to students); the first passage has **Cierto/Falso** questions and the second has short-answer questions (Student Supplement, p. 21).

1. Me llamo Carlos Padilla. Soy estudiante de arquitectura en la Universidad de México (UNAM), aquí en el Distrito Federal. Tengo veintiún años y vivo con mis padres en la Calle Juárez, en el sur de la ciudad. Tengo ojos negros y pelo moreno. Tengo dos hermanas y un hermano. También tengo un perro que se llama Sultán.

   CIERTO/FALSO

   1. Carlos estudia en la Universidad de los Andes.
   2. Vive en la Calle 18.
   3. Tiene ojos negros.
   4. Tiene dos hermanos y una hermana.
   5. Tiene dos perros.

2. Catalina trabaja para pagar los libros y la matrícula este semestre. Ella trabaja en un supermercado desde las ocho de la mañana hasta las 12:00 del mediodía. El Sr. Hernández compra comida para su familia allí todos los días. Los hijos necesitan mucha comida. "Cómo está la familia?" pregunta Catalina. "Bien, gracias," contesta el Sr. Hernández. Hay 6 personas en la familia del Sr. Hernández: la esposa, Elena, un hijo y 3 hijas. Hay un perro en la familia también. El perro se llama Rambo. "¿Papel o plástico?" pregunta Catalina. "Papel, por favor", contesta el Sr. Hernández. El Sr. Hernández trabaja en IBM y la Sra. Hernández trabaja en 3M. Los dos trabajan porque hay muchos gastos con 4 hijos. "Hasta luego",dice Catalina. "Adiós", dice el Sr. Hernández.

   1. ¿Compra el Sr. Hernández la comida por la mañana o por la tarde?
   2. ¿Cómo se llama la esposa del Sr. Hernández?
   3. ¿Cuántas hijas hay en la familia Hernández?
   4. ¿Cómo se llama el perro?
   5. ¿Dónde trabaja Catalina? ¿Por qué?
   6. ¿Dónde trabaja el Sr. Hernández? ¿Y su esposa?

E. Family Tree Diagram. (Student Supplement, p. 22) Tell the class that you are going to read a description of a family and that they must fill in the information as you go along. They will be filling in names and ages. Here is the description (after reading it to your class, you can verify comprehension by putting the diagram up on the board and filling in the information as a group).

Los abuelos de la familia se llaman Carlos y María. Carlos tiene 72 años y María tiene 64. Viven en San Antonio. En total, tienen 4 hijos: 3 varones y una mujer. Desgraciadamente, uno de los hijos murió en un accidente. El hijo muerto se llamaba Pedro. Otro de los hijos de Carlos y María está divorciado. Se llama Ramón, tiene 32 años y es periodista para el Dallas Morning News. La ex-esposa de Ramón se llama Ana. Ana y Ramón tienen una hija, Beatriz. Ella tiene 10 años y vive con su mamá en California. Pero todos los años durante las vacaciones Beatriz va a Texas para visitar a su papá y también a su única prima, Carmen. Carmen tiene 9 años. Ella y Beatriz son muy buenas amigas. Carmen y Beatriz tienen dos primos también: se llaman Carlitos y Raúl. Viven en San Antonio con sus padres Mercedes y José Luis. Mercedes tiene 36 años y es profesora. José Luis es un poco mayor; él tiene 43 años y es abogado. José Luis tiene una hermana. Ella se llama Isabel; tiene 35 años y ahora está embarazada. Va a tener un bebé en marzo. Isabel y su esposo Manolo están muy contentos. También su hija Carmen está contenta porque a ella le gustan mucho los bebés. Cuando el bebé nazca en marzo, toda la familia va a tener una fiesta grande en San Antonio.

III. GRAMMAR.

The following worksheets are in the Student Supplement.

A. Las nacionalidades. (p. 23) Practices with adjectives of nationality and geography.

B. ¿Cómo es esta familia? (p. 24) This is a good practice with family vocabulary and adjectives.

C. Descripciones y preguntas. (p. 25) This picture-based worksheet practices with adjectives and question formation.

D. Explaining your reasons. (p. 26) A series of personal questions soliciting **porque** and **para** + *infinitive* in the answers.

E. Sopa de verbos. (p. 27) Two cloze passages, reviewing **-ar**, **-er**, and **-ir** verbs.

F. Ensalada de verbos y adjetivos. (p. 28) A cloze passage.

G. Repaso. (pp. 29-31) Covers the main vocabulary, grammar, and communicative functions of Chapter 2.

IV. INTEGRATIVE ACTIVITIES.

At this point, we encourage you to provide ample speaking opportunities for your students. Here are several integrative activities and games which lend themselves to plenty of verbal exchange.

A. "Mi familia" Presentations. After presenting the Chapter 2 vocabulary to the class, tell your students that you are now going to talk about your own family Bring in pictures of your relatives and give the class a brief description of your family, supplementing your talk with a diagram on the chalkboard. Then tell the class that each student is to give a brief (3 min.) talk about his/her family. Encourage them to bring photos or ask them to draw pictures. This is one of the most enjoyable activities of the semester, which you can do in one of two ways:

1. Each day set aside time for 5-6 presentations with some follow-up questions afterwards. Depending on the size of your class, it will take 4-5 days to do all of the presentations.
2. Divide the class into groups of 5-6 students and have them do their presentations within the group. Circulate and monitor progress.

B. Una familia imaginaria. Using magazine pictures (your own or pictures your students can bring in), create an imaginary family. Tape pictures to the chalkboard, starting with the abuelos and working your way through. Solicit class opinions as you go. Ask the class: "¿Quién es él? ¿Cómo se llama? ¿Es casado o soltero? ¿Tiene hijos?" etc. Include some details on the chalkboard. This is an excellent way to review structures such as "¿Cómo se llama? ¿Cómo es?" as well as presenting new structures such as "¿Cuántos años tiene?" Encourage students to be as imaginative as possible in their ideas about the family and use class responses to introduce unfamiliar vocabulary such as: **divorciado, muerto, embarazada, viudo, yerno, cuñado/a, nuera,** etc.

C. Associations. Practice vocabulary and adjectival agreement by asking the class what adjectives they associate with famous people. You can use the list from the Chapter 1 supplement, tailoring it to the personality of your own class.

D. Class poll. "El hombre ideal/La mujer ideal." This is a fun activity. Divide the chalkboard into two halves and write "El hombre ideal" at the top of the first half and "La mujer ideal" at the top of the second. Then start soliciting class opinions, writing down the information on the chalkboard as you go. For example: "James, en tu opinión, ¿cómo es la mujer ideal?" ¿Qué profesión tiene? ¿Cuántos años tiene? etc. There are all kinds of questions you can ask; this is a good review activity. See how many different opinions you can get as a class and compare them. Ask if the ideal man or woman exists.

E. El horóscopo y el carácter. The Student Supplement includes a horoscope handout and a reading comprehension worksheet (Student Supplement, pp. 32-33). If you choose, you may assign this as a reading assignment the night before class discussion; you may also skip having the students do a preliminary reading before class and lead right into the discussion instead. Begin a group discussion of the sheet. Ask questions such as:

1. ¿Cuáles son las fechas para Piscis? ¿Aries? ¿Libra? etc.
2. ¿Cuáles son dos características de Acuario? ¿Leo? etc.
3. ¿Quiénes en esta clase son sagitarios? ¿Mary? Mary, ¿cuántos años tienes?
4. ¿Y cuándo es tu cumpleaños? ¿Es verdad que tú eres entusiasta y optimista? ¿Cómo eres?

After asking some of the types of questions above, ask the other students if the description given of a particular sign is true for one of the students of that sign. For example: "Helen, ¿cuál es tu signo? ¿Tauro? ¿Entonces eres temperamental?" "Clase, ¿piensan Uds. que Helen es temperamental ? ¿No? ¿Cómo es ella, entonces?" Another possibility is to describe yourself and then have the class guess your sign.

F. Dialogue Practice. Cut out pictures of odd-looking people who will be members of a weird family. There should be a grandfather, a mother, a father, a younger child, a teenage girl and the boyfriend of the teenage girl.

Tape the pictures of these family members to the board; spend a couple of minutes talking about their identities: "¿Quién es el abuelo? ¿Cómo se llama la madre? ¿Cómo se llaman los dos hijos menores?" Then tell the class that the **hija mayor** has a new **amigo** to introduce to the family. Assign identities to 3-4 students: "John, tú eres el papá. Gwen, tú eres la mamá. Sharon, tú eres la hija mayor y, Peter, tú eres al amigo nuevo." Have them role-play and perform the introductions using the expressions on p. 81. Change groups 2-3 times to get students as familiar as possible with these expressions and point out that the new **amigo** would use a different expression when speaking to the **abuelo** than when meeting the **hija menor**.

Then refer the students to pp. 81-82 of Puntos. Break them up into groups of 3-4 people and tell them that they are to create a dialogue based on one of the situations. Encourage them to use their imaginations. Again, the same guidelines apply as in the Chapter 1 Teacher's Guide: Give the students 5 min. to create the dialogue, and after the presentations spend some time on the correction of common errors.

G. Communicative Goals Practice #1. (Student Supplement, p. 35) Beginning in Chapter 2 and appearing every four chapters throughout the Student Supplement, we have included Communicative Goals practices for students. These practices consist of a picture, thematically related to the chapter, instructions for students, and a list of suggested Communicative Goals to use with the picture. Essentially, the purpose of these practices is to get students to describe the pictures in a limited amount of time, using as many of the listed goals as they can. They serve as a reminder to students of what they have been learning so far in the semester.

There are several different ways to use these practices. They are excellent as rehearsal for mid-semester or final oral interviews. They may also be used in-class as paired speaking practice, with students describing the drawings to each other. Have partners ask one another questions about the drawing after their descriptions. They may also be used as a whole-class speaking practice and review of goals. Assign the practice as homework, and the next day in class, put the picture and listed goals up on a transparency. Call on different students to give their descriptions corresponding to the numbered goals.

V. GAMES

A. Password and Pictionary. Please refer to pp. 9-10 of the Chapter 1 Teacher's Guide for instructions. Both games work well as vocabulary review, especially toward the end of chapters.

B. Bingo "La familia". (Student Supplement, p. 34) This bingo can be used in the same way as the "Gustar" bingo in Chapter 1. This is a good way for students to practice getting and giving information about their families.

C. The Family Reunion Game. Please see the instruction sheet and sample information cards on the following two pages.

THE FAMILY REUNION GAME

This exercise gives the students new identities, gets them moving around the classroom and talking with many other students. There doesn't seem to be a temptation to use English because the information is geared to their level. Furthermore, the exercise reflects that comprehension is easier than production in a second language. This exercise is a lot of fun and successfully promotes speaking. Doing this early in the semester facilitates interaction and breaks down inhibitions.

There are three families in the room. Put the information for each person on a 3 x 5 card which can be used every year. Everyone in the room gets a card with their name, something about themselves, and a clue about another family member whom they must look for. For example:

> Usted se llama Susana.
> A usted le gusta tomar mucho coñac.
> Usted es de Los Angeles.
> Su hermano es antropólogo.
> Él estudia gorilas en Africa.

They have a couple of minutes to memorize the information. They then go around the room trying to locate their family members. For example, Susana asks all the men in the room if they study gorillas in Africa and if they are anthropologists. Once she finds her brother (she discovers his name is Jorge), she can help him find their mother, whom he is looking for. At the same time David, a movie star who lives in Los Angeles, is looking for his wife. He knows she also lives in Los Angeles and that she is an alcoholic. As you can see, he is looking for Susana.

You may have to invent another family or other family members on your own so that you will have the right number of men and women for your class. These (*detachable people) tend to be the last to unite with the family since they are looking for someone, but no one is looking for them. If they become discouraged or complain that no one wants them, ask them: "¿A quién buscas? ¿A tu padre? Ah, pobrecito, tal vez eres un huérfano."

The first group united for a family reunion wins. Ask this family questions in Spanish while the others are still looking for their family members. They all have things to say about the family: **¿Quién es usted? ¿Es casado? ¿Tiene hijos? ¿Cómo son? ¿Quién es tu madre?**

The assumed identities, which are purposely exaggerated characters, reduce the concern with ego. Due to the element of competition, students are eager to communicate in Spanish. Because everyone is chattering away in Spanish at once, even the most inhibited student jump into the fray.

I. PRIMERA FAMILIA

Ud. se llama PABLO
Ud. es profesor en Harvard
Ud. es de Boston
A su nieto no le gusta estudiar
Él tiene catorce años

Ud. se llama CATALINA
Ud. es médica
Ud. es de Boston
Su esposo es profesor de Harvard
Él también es de Boston

Te llamas VALENTÍN
Tu familia es rica pero eres pobre
Vives en el metro de Nueva York
Tú mamá es médica
Ella está en Boston

Ud. se llama VICTORIA
Ud. es bibliotecaria
Ud. vive en Nueva Jersey
Su hermano está en N.Y.
Él no es parte de la familia

Ud. se llama EDUARDO
Ud. vive en Nueva Jersey
Ud. es un actor de películas
Su esposa es bibliotecaria
Ella también vive en N.J.

Te llamas CARLOS
Tienes catorce años
No te gusta estudiar
Tu padre es un actor de películas
Vives con él en Nueva Jersey

(OPTIONAL RELATIVES)

II. SEGUNDA FAMILIA

Ud. se llama RUDY
Ud. es el presidente de EXXON
Ud. es de Houston
Su nieta tiene once años
Ella mira televisión mucho

Ud. se llama MARÍA
Ud. no trabaja, es rica
Le gustan los animales exóticos
Su esposo es de Houston
Él es el presidente de EXXON

Ud. se llama JORGE
Ud. estudia gorilas en Africa
Ud. es antropólogo
Su madre es rica
Le gustan los animales exóticos.

Ud. se llama SUSANA
Ud. toma mucho coñac
Ud. es de Los Ángeles
Su hermano es antropólogo
Él estudia gorilas en Africa

Ud. se llama DAVÍD
Ud. es de Los Ángeles
Ud. trabaja en una Co. de botas
Su esposa es alcohólica
Ella es de Los Ángeles

Te llamas RAQUEL
Te gusta mirar televisión
Tienes once años
Tu padre trabaja en una
compañía de botas
Vives con él en Los Ángeles

Te llamas ALEJANDRA
Tomas mucha Coca-cola
Tienes cinco años
Tu abuela es rica
Le gustan los animales exóticos

III. TERCERA FAMILIA

Ud. se llama CONCHA
Ud. tiene un rancho
Ud. es de Llano, Texas
Su hijo vive en Austin
Él estudia medicina en UT

Ud. se llama PEDRO
Ud. inventa cosas
Vive en Llano, Texas
Su esposa tiene un rancho
Ella también es de Llano.

Ud. se llama MARÍA
Ud. es directora de un museo de arte
Ud. es de Austin, Texas
Su esposo vive en Austin también
Él estudia medicina

Ud. se llama MANUEL
Ud. vive en Austin, Texas
Ud. estudia medicina
Tu hermana vive en Austin
Ella trabaja con computadoras

Ud. se llama ELENA
Ud. vive en Austin, Texas
Ud. trabaja con computadoras
Su padre es de Llano, Texas
Él es muy inteligente, inventa cosas

Te llamas ESTEBAN (optional)
Te gustan los coches de plástico
Tienes cuatro años
Vives en Austin con tu mamá
Ella es directora de un museo de arte

Te llamas JUANA
Te gusta andar en bicicleta
Tienes ocho años
Tu abuelo es muy inteligente
Él inventa cosas

CAPÍTULO 3

Communicative Goals for Chapter 3
By the end of the chapter students should be able to:

- * discuss clothing and shopping ☐
- * ask for and give prices ☐
- * tell what belongs to you and others ☐
- * discuss preferences and wishes ☐
- * talk about the future ☐

Grammatical Structures
Students should know:

- * stem-changing verbs ☐
- * **tener** idioms ☐
- * **ir** + **a** + infinitive ☐
- * possessive adjectives ☐
- * contraction **al** ☐

I. PRONUNCIATION

Don't forget to remind students to use visualization and association when learning vocabulary. It's a good idea to combine new vocabulary and pronunciation practice. The following pronunciation/vocabulary drill is on p. 37 of the Student Supplement.

A. Pronounce the following groups of words; have students repeat the words and then ask them to visualize the object:

los zapatos azules	la lana de Londres	la bolsa bonita	el almacén allá
la cartera de cuero	la revista rosada	la puerta parda	las rayas rojas

B. For further practice, some verses of the children's poem "La gata maroma" appear on p. 37 of the Student Supplement.

II. LISTENING COMPREHENSION.

Try to include some form of listening comprehension activity daily. Here are five possibilities.

A. Preguntas personales. This can be done as a warm-up activity; form your questions based on the vocabulary and structures of Chapter 3. You can also include questions relating to previous chapters to help students review or refresh their memories. Here are some possibilities for Chapter 3.

1. ¿Dónde te gusta comprar ropa?
2. ¿Qué tipo de ropa venden en (*name of store*)?
3. Cuando vas de compras, ¿siempre buscas las rebajas?
4. ¿Usas una tarjeta de crédito para comprar ropa?
5. ¿Qué ropa prefieres llevar a clase? ¿a una fiesta?
6. ¿Cuántas corbatas tienes? ¿Te gusta llevar corbatas?
7. ¿Cuántos pares de zapatos tienes?
8. ¿Qué artículo de ropa quieres comprar pronto?
9. ¿Cuáles son más grandes, mis zapatos, tus zapatos o sus (*point to another student*) zapatos? ¿Cuál es más bonita, mi camiseta o tu camiseta?
10. ¿Puedes ir de compras esta tarde? ¿Qué vas a hacer esta tarde?
11. ¿Tienes que estudiar esta noche?

12. ¿Tienes sueño ahora? ¿Vas a tomar una siesta más tarde?
13. ¿Prefieres las clases por la mañana o por la tarde?
14. ¿Tienes ganas de tomar un café después de clase? ¿Qué tienes ganas de hacer mañana?
15. ¿Tienes miedo de las cucarachas? ¿de los exámenes? ¿de la profesora de español?

B. True/False and Multiple-Choice Statements. Read these sentences aloud as a practice or pop quiz activity. Verify comprehension afterwards. Here are some possible true/false statements for Chapter 3.

1. Es necesario llevar una corbata a la clase de español.
2. Las camisetas y los pantalones cortos son ropa apropriada para la playa.
3. En el Canadá en diciembre las personas llevan sandalias y trajes de baño.
4. Se vende ropa de última moda en los cafés.
5. Si no tienes mucho dinero para comprar ropa, debes buscar las gangas.
6. Una blusa de seda cuesta más que una camiseta de algodón.
7. Unas personas supersticiosas tienen miedo de los gatos negros.

Multiple Choice:

1. Los precios en los almacenes son muy altos. Por ejemplo, un traje de seda de Chanel cuesta aproximadamente: a) $5.500 b) $700 c) $79.
2. Si Ud. tiene un examen mañana en la clase de historia, pero esta noche Ud. no estudia y va al cine con unos amigos, entonces mañana Ud. va a tener: a) razón b) un gran problema c) prisa.
3. Antes del examen final, los estudiantes deben: a) salir con sus amigos para bailar b) estudiar c) leer una novela romántica.
4. Este fin de semana tengo que ir a Chicago en coche. No estoy contento/a porque: a) no tengo ganas de hacer el viaje b) tengo mucho miedo de los aviones c) tengo razón.
5. Estás en el mercado en Palenque, México. Quieres comprarle unas sandalias a tu amiga Isabel, pero las sandalias que te gustan cuestan demasiado. ¿Qué le dices al vendedor? a) ¿Se aceptan tarjetas de crédito? b) ¡Estas sandalias son de última moda! c) Creo que necesito algo más barato.
6. ¡Qué suerte! Vas a pasar las vacaciones de marzo esquiando en las montañas de Colorado. Necesitas llevar contigo un abrigo, un suéter de lana y: a) un cinturón de cuero b) una bolsa c) un par de botas.
7. Tu amigo Carlos cree que la música "rap" va a ser popular por muchos años. En tu opinión, esa música es horrible. ¿Qué le dices a tu amigo? a) Carlos, no tienes razón. b) Carlos, ¿tienes mucha prisa? c) Carlos, eres un imbécil; ya no somos amigos.

C. Definiciones. Now that we are in Chapter 3, students can begin to produce language in addition to responding to what they hear. Read these definitions and have students write the word being defined.

1. El artículo de ropa que usamos/llevamos cuando nadamos.
2. Un lugar donde venden de todo.

3. Un tipo de zapato informal que llevamos en el verano cuando hace calor, con pantalones cortos, o para ir a la playa.
4. El artículo de ropa que llevamos cuando llueve (un tipo de abrigo).
5. Un artículo de ropa largo y delgado que los hombres de negocios llevan con los trajes.
6. El artículo de ropa que llevamos dentro de los zapatos.
7. Un tipo de zapato que llevamos cuando hace frío o cuando llueve y que pueden ser de cuero o de plástico.
8. El lugar donde hay muchas tiendas y una plaza de aparcamiento enorme.

D. El inventorio del Almacén Matilde. Have students complete the chart on p. 38 of the Student Supplement.

INSTRUCTIONS (read to students):
You will hear a list of clothing items, the number of each item left in the store at the end of the year, and the price of each item. Fill in the chart with the information.

1. calcetines de rayas azules y amarillas, 92 pares, 675 pesetas c/u.
2. impermeables de plástico para señoras, 367, 2.499 pesetas c/u.
3. corbatas de seda moradas y anaranjadas, 1.534, 3.875 pesetas c/u.
4. minifaldas de cuadros, 906, 5.560 pesetas c/u.
5. relojes marca Rolex, 11, 580.000 pesetas c/u.
6. zapatos de tacón alto para señoras, 72 pares, 11.700 pesetas c/u.

E. En la tienda Zara. Read to the students the prices of the articles of clothing pictured on p. 38 of the Student Supplement. Have students write the price next to the corresponding item of clothing.

1. camisa: 4.225 pts.
2. blusa 6.900 pts.
3. bufanda: 1.400 pts.
4. falda: 6.315 pts.
5. vestido: 7.770 pts.
6. sombrero: 3.195 pts.
7. pantalones para hombre: 8.750 pts.
8. zapatos para hombre: 10.500 pts.
9. abrigo para hombre: 15.295 pts.
10. guantes: 4.350 pts.
11. suéter para señora: 5.400 pts.
12. botas para señora: 11.790 pts.

F. El horario. This is a combination listening comprehension problem-solving activity. A copy of the blank schedule is in the Student Supplement on p. 39. Read out the schedule below to the class. Students fill in the schedule with the information in order to determine when the four people in the passage can get together for a study session. (NOTE: This activity is a little more fun if you create your own schedule using 4-5 students from the class and their daily activities.) After the passage is read, verify comprehension.

Cuatro estudiantes -- María, Juan, José y Sara -- quieren reunirse para estudiar para su examen de español. Cada estudiante tiene un horario diferente. Llena el horario con la información necesaria para averiguar cuándo se pueden reunir por dos horas para estudiar.

Todos los estudiantes están en la clase de español desde las doce hasta la una de la tarde. José tiene su clase de biología inmediatamente antes de la clase de español. Sara almuerza en la cafetería desde la una hasta las dos de la tarde todos los días con su novio. A María le gusta bailar y por eso ella no se puede reunir después de las cuatro porque tiene clase de ballet. Juan necesita ganar dinero para pagar la matrícula y por eso trabaja por las mañanas de las 8:00 de la mañana a las 12:00. Sara estudia y lee sus libros de antropología en la biblioteca todas las mañanas de las nueve hasta las once. José juega baloncesto todas las noches en el gimnasio con Juan después de las cinco de la tarde.

¿Cuándo pueden reunirse los cuatro estudiantes por dos horas para estudiar para su examen de español?

III. GRAMMAR

Students get a lot of grammar in this chapter, especially new verb structures. The following worksheets are in the Student Supplement.

A. ¿De quién son estas cosas? This art-based practice incorporates clothing vocabulary, possession with **ser**, and possessive adjectives. (p. 40)

B. Los posesivos. Two cloze passages. (p. 41)

C. Prepositions and contractions. This fill-in-the-blank worksheet reviews prepositions and contractions from earlier chapters and Chapter 3. (p. 43)

D. Verb worksheet. A translation practice that helps students distinguish between the different verb-infinitive combinations. It can be assigned as homework or done in class, with each student responsible for putting a sentence on the board. (p. 43)

E. Ensalada gramatical. A cloze passage practicing verbs, articles, possessives, agreement, and vocabulary. Great for review. (p. 45)

F. Planes y preferencias. This sentence-building practice works with the different verb-infinitive combinations. (p. 45)

G. Repaso. This is a good handout for test review. (pp. 46-48)

H. Error-Correction Sheet. Start collecting errors from compositions, quizzes, dialogues, etc. Distribute a list of 15-20 sentences of common errors to the class on a worksheet, and have students correct the sentences. Focus on common errors, such as agreement, adjective placement and problems with **gustar**. Have each student write one corrected sentence on the board and ask classmates to verify corrections. Here are some samples:

1. Vamos mirar una película.
2. Llevo los pantalones corto blanco.
3. Tengo ojos verde y pequeña.
4. También llego zapatos de tenis.
5. Vamos a la restaurante francés.
6. ¿Quieres tocar básquetbol?
7. La blusa y la falda son algodón.
8. Mis pantalones es el color azul.
9. Mis ojos son azul.
10. Me llama Dave.
11. Vamos al restaurante italiana.
12. Tengo alta.
13. ¿Tienes ganas de comes comida mexicana?
14. Soy llevo un suéter de rayas.
15. Vamos ir a una discoteca.

IV. INTEGRATIVE ACTIVITIES

A. Busca a alguien que... (Student Supplement, p. 49) This is a fun activity that practices question formation and noun-adjective agreement.

B. Entrevistas: el futuro. (Student Supplement, p. 50) Students ask each other about future plans, using the **ir + a + infinitive** structure. This is a good activity after the students have been formally introduced to **ir + a + infinitive**. It's also a good idea to have the class as a group report on some of their findings afterwards.

C. ¿Cuál es el regalo perfecto? Divide students into pairs and have them complete the information-gap activity on p. 51 of the Student Supplement. Instruct students to cover up their partners' charts as they gather information. When they've completed their charts, students decide together what gifts to buy for different people, based on the information they have gathered.

D. Diálogos y situaciones. *Puntos* contains some good situations on p. 110; before having the students write their diálogos, introduce the vocabulary in the **Situación** on p. 110. You may want to model a dialogue with a student for the class.By now your students should be accustomed to creating a reasonable conversatin in a short period of time. Encourage them to think on their feet instead of relying on a written script. As always, allow a few moments of class time after the presentations to hammer out some common errors.

E. Clothing Description Activity. Have students bring in a picture from the Sunday ads or from a catalogue of someone dressed in interesting clothes. In pairs, have one student describe his/her ad to the other student without revealing the ad. The second student draws what s/he hears described. After the pair finished describing and drawing the ad, they compare the original ad with the drawing to see how they match. Partners then switch roles.

F. Guided Writing. Staring in Chapter 3, every chapter will include a Guided Writing activity that consists of three parts:

1) A series of ten questions (posed in English so that the structures are not merely copied from the question) which students answer in Spanish for homework. The next day have ten students each put one answer on the board. Correct their errors and as each sentence is checked, ask a different student to tell you in Spanish what the question was.

2) After reviewing answers, have the class prepare short, spontaneous dialogues between any two or three characters in the drawing. These dialogues should not be written. Ask a few groups to perform for the class.

3) As a follow-up, have students write a letter of about 100 words from one of the people pictured in the drawing to a family member. In their letters, students should use the vocabulary and grammar structures that they practiced in Parts 1 and 2. See p. 52 of the Student Supplement for the Chapter 3 picture and questions.

V. GAMES

A. 20 Questions/20 Preguntas. This game works well for practicing agreement and Chapter 3 vocabulary. Here are the rules:

One student comes to the front of the class and thinks of another student in the class. Classmates ask yes/no questions until they guess who the student is. This game can be played with famous people, too. However, for Chapter 3 using classmates allows students to practice clothing and colors.

EXAMPLE: ¿Es una mujer? ¿Es rubia? ¿Es alta? ¿Lleva pantalones hoy? ¿Es Mónica?

Have the students take turns asking questions by row. This allows everyone to participate and prevents the student who identifies the person immediately from getting the answer so quickly.

B. Picture Identification. Have each student bring in a magazine picture of a person (tell them it must be large and/or easy to distinguish), onto which they attach a full description of that person (appearance, clothing, etc.). Look over the sentences that night and correct the errors. The next day in class give back the descriptions but keep the pictures. Give the students 2-3 minutes to look over your corrections while you tape up the magazine pictures on the chalkboard(s). Label each picture with a number.

Divide the class into 2 groups. One student from Team A reads his/her description aloud to a student from Team B or to Team B as a whole. Team B listens, looks at the pictures and then attempts to identify the person being described. If Team B identifies correctly, they win a point and the picture is removed from the board. If not, Team A has an opportunity to guess. After each picture is identified, remove it from the board. As a variation, read the descriptions to the class after having taped up and labeled the pictures. Students listen and when called on by you, attempt to identify the pictures and get a point for their team.

CAPÍTULO 4

Communicative Goals for Chapter 4
By the end of the chapter students should be able to:

* discuss weekly and daily routines	☐
* describe where they live	☐
* point out people and things	☐

Grammatical Structures
Students should know:

* more stem-changing verbs	☐
* reflexive pronouns	☐
* demonstrative adjectives	☐

I. PRONUNCIATION

A. See the top of p. 53 in the Student Supplement for pronunciation practice. The sentences are here as well.

1. Esta semana salgo con Víctor Vásquez el viernes, César Serrat el sábado y Diana Dolores del Duero el domingo.
2. Las sicólogos suecas, Sara y Susana, venden sillones, sofás y sillas super-sofisticadas.
3. Conchita Correa quiere comprar una casa en Ceres con comedor cómodo y cama de agua.
4. Pablo y Pilar piensan poner unos pocos preciosos platos portugueses en las paredes y unas plantas pequeñas en el patio.

B. For more practice with the b and v sounds, see the proverbs on p. 53 of the Student Supplement.

II. LISTENING COMPREHENSION

A. Preguntas personales. These work well when used as a warm-up activity, quick vocabulary review, and lead-ins to other activities.

1. ¿A qué hora te despiertas durante la semana? ¿Y los fines de semana?
2. ¿Siempre te acuestas tarde los viernes y los sábados?
3. ¿Qué haces cuando no puedes dormirte?
4. ¿Te gusta leer mientras te bañas? ¿Y cantar mientras te duchas?
5. ¿Quién aquí puede ducharse y vestirse en menos de 10 minutos? ¿Cuánto tiempo necesitas para ducharte y vestirte?
6. Cuando te vistes, ¿piensas primero en la comodidad o en la moda?
7. ¿Cuál es más desagradable, afeitarse las piernas o la barba?
8. Te llamas __________, ¿verdad? ¿Tu mamá/Tu papá también se llama así? ¿Hay otras personas en tu familia con ese mismo nombre?
9. ¿Qué haces para divertirte?
10. ¿Te diviertes en la clase de español? ¿Y en la clase de __________?
11. ¿Prefieres levantarte temprano o tarde? ¿Por qué?
12. ¿Qué haces inmediatamente después de levantarte?
13. ¿Qué te pones cuando quieres vestirte bien?
14. ¿En qué parte de la casa te sientas cuando quieres estar cómodo/a?
15. ¿En qué parte de la casa te acuestas para tomar una siesta?

Here are some groups of questions focusing on reflexive vs. non-reflexive actions and on placement of reflexive pronouns.

1. ¿Qué tipo de ropa te pones para una fiesta elegante?
2. ¿Siempre pones tu ropa en el armario?
3. ¿Puedes dormirte si tienes un examen al día siguiente?
4. ¿En qué cuarto de la casa duermes?
5. ¿Te gusta cantar mientras te bañas?
6. ¿Quién tiene un perro? ¿Bañas a tu perro todas las semanas?
7. ¿Prefieres acostarte temprano o tarde durante la semana?
8. ¿Piensas que los padres deben acostar a sus hijos temprano?
9. ¿Te vistes bien para salir con tus amigos? ¿Para ir a una fiesta?
10. Las madres tienen que vestir a sus hijos pequeños. ¿Por qué?
11. ¿A qué hora te despiertas durante la semana? ¿Y los fines de semana?
12. ¿Es necesario despertar a tu compañero de cuarto a veces?
13. ¿Te afeitas cada día?
14. ¿Te gusta afeitarte?
15. ¿Nos divertimos en la clase de español?
16. ¿Es posible divertirse durante un examen?
17. ¿Dónde prefieres sentarte en la clase de español?
18. En un concierto, ¿te gusta sentarte o levantarte para escuchar la música?
19. ¿Te duchas antes o después de tomar un café por la mañana?

B. Definitions. Use statements like these for warm-up, daily listening comprehension practice, or vocabulary review.

1. El lugar donde dan peliculas.
2. El día después de mañana es __________.
3. La parte de la semana cuando no hay clases y cuando podemos descansar y hacer las cosas que nos gustan.
4. Una silla muy grande y cómoda.
5. El lugar donde se ponen los libros.
6. Un líquido que se hace de frutas y que se toma frecuentemente por la mañana.
7. El lugar donde se aparca el coche.
8. Si hoy es miércoles, pasado mañana es __________.
9. Un juego complicado e intelectual en que se usan piezas blancas y negras.
10. Lo opuesto de ponerse la ropa.
11. Lo opuesto de despertarse.
12. Si no tienes mucho tiempo, es mejor ducharte; pero si tienes tiempo y quieres relajarte, puedes __________.

C. True/False Statements.

1. Si hoy es jueves, pasado mañano es miércoles.
2. El lunes es el día después del domingo.
3. La gente se baña en la cocina.
4. Por lo general, te levantas después de despertarte.

5. En una casa típica, los armarios están en la sala.
6. Es buena idea poner leche y refrescos en una cómoda.
7. Los estudiantes están muy contentos los lunes y muy tristes los viernes.

D. Description: Una casa nueva. Read the script below to students while they complete the chart on the bottom of p. 54 in the Student Supplement.

You will hear a friend describing her plans for furnishing her new house. On the left, list what she and her housemate already have for the house; on the right, list what they still need.

Yo ya tengo un sofá y dos sillones para la sala, pero no tengo ninguna mesita para las lámparas. Va a ser necesario comprar unos estantes para todos nuestros libros. La cocina tiene refrigerador, estufa y lavaplatos; tal vez podemos comprar una lavadora a segunda mano. Las dos tenemos camas, pero necesitamos buscar unas alfombras para el comedor y las dos alcobas. El aire acondicionador de la sala no funciona muy bien; creo que vamos a tener que arreglarlo o comprar uno nuevo.

E. La rutina de Chela. Read the script below to students while they complete the chart and do the true/false questions on p. 54 of the Student Supplement. The first time you read, have students complete the chart; the second time, students should listen for the answers to the true/ false questions.

Mi rutina diaria nunca es exactamente igual, pues cambia un poco según el día de la semana. Los días de entresemana, estoy muy ocupada con mi trabajo, mis clases y mi familia. Por lo general, durante la semana me acuesto a las once o las once y media. Pongo el despertador para las siete, pero típicamente no me levanto hasta las siete y media. Me gustan los fines de semana porque puedo dormir un poco más. Los domingos, me despierto a las ocho y cuarto, y no me levanto hasta las ocho y media o las nueve menos cuarto. Durante la semana, casi siempre tengo prisa por la mañana. Así que me ducho rápidamente y me visto a las ocho, más o menos. A veces ni tengo tiempo para sentarme a tomar un café, porque necesito estar en mi oficina en la universidad a las nueve menos cuarto. Pero los domingos es todo lo contrario; no tengo prisa y después de levantarme, voy a la cocina, me preparo un café con leche y un buen desayuno. Después, me siento tranquilamente en el comedor para leer el periódico de nueve a diez. Más tarde, a eso de las diez y media, me ducho y me visto. Lo único malo de los domingos es que el día siguiente es lunes. Por eso, me tengo que acostar temprano, como a las diez o las diez y media.

F. Dictado. Dictations are an excellent listening practice if the sentences are read in "chunks" of at least three words at a time. One suggestion is to have one student go to the side blackboard while the others do the dictation at their seats. Check each sentence right away. Read the sentence once as indicated, tell students the number of words in the sentence, then repeat it once more.

1. El sábado casi siempre / me levanto tarde, / me baño, me visto / y salgo con los amigos / para almorzar. (18)
2. Cecilia se viste / de moda, / pero Pablito se pone / cualquier cosa. (11)

3. En mi casa, / el sillón y el sofá / son los lugares más cómodos / para sentarse. (15)
4. El viernes, / Víctor Vásquez / vuelve a ver / a Verónica, / su amiga venezolana. (12)

III. GRAMMAR

A. Práctica de verbos. (p. 55) This contextualized worksheet practices new Chapter 4 verbs, as well as old ones.

B. Los verbos nuevos: Irregular and Stem-changing. (p. 56) A series of short cloze passages.

C. Ensalada gramatical I: Stem-changing verbs. (p. 57) Three cloze passages practicing verbs and some possessives, demonstratives, and adjectives.

D. Ensalada gramatical II: Un lunes difícil para Pepe. (p. 58) A longer cloze passage with follow-up questions.

E. Reflexive Actions. (p. 59) Two cloze passages

F. Reflexive Actions: Description. (p. 60) Have students use the drawing as a good global reflexives practice.

G. Demonstrative Adjectives. (p. 61) Two cloze passages.

H. Repaso. (pages 62-64)

I. Sample verb quizzes. The following 4 cloze passages can be used as short quizzes or as a review for Chapter 4 material.

1. Este semestre el lunes es el peor día de la semana para mí. Yo ________________ (*get up*) temprano y ____________________ (*spend*) la mañana en la universidad. A las dos ____________________ (*I go*) al trabajo. Por la noche ________________ (*I return*) a la casa, ____________________ (*I put on*) el televisor, ______________ (*I sit down*) a estudiar, pero siempre ____________________ (*I fall asleep*) dentro de veinte minutos. A la una ____________________ (*I wake up*), ______________ (*go up*) a mi cuarto, ______________ (*wash*) la cara y ________________ (*go to bed*).

¿Por qué está cansada esta persona los lunes?

2. La vida de Pedro Perezoso: __________________ (*He looks for*) trabajo el lunes, __________________ (*he finds*) un trabajo el martes, __________________ (*he loses*) el trabajo el miércoles, __________________ (*he receives*) un cheque pequeño el jueves, __________________ (*he spends*) el dinero el viernes, el sábado ________________ (*he doesn't do*) nada y el domingo ________________ (*he rests*).

¿Por qué recibe Pedro un cheque pequeño?

3. Por la mañana Julio y Mari ____________________ (*wake up*) a las siete, ____________________ (*they prepare*) el café, ____________________ (*they look for*) el periódico y ____________________ (*they sit down*) a leerlo. Cuando ellos ____________________ (*finish*) el periódico, Julio ____________________ (*bathes*) y Mari ____________ (*washes*) los platos. Julio ____________ (*gets dressed*) rápidamente mientras Mari ____________ (*takes a shower*). Los dos ____________ (*leave*) de la casa a las ocho y media y ____________ (*go*) al trabajo. Nunca ____________ (*arrive*) tarde.

¿Qué hacen Julio y Mari antes de bañarse?

IV. INTEGRATIVE ACTIVITIES

A. "Se vende/se alquila casa." This activity combines reading, writing, and listening skills. Begin by looking over the classified housing ads on p. 147 of *Puntos*. Ask students to find places appropriate or not appropriate for someone who likes sports, someone with a large family, someone who likes privacy, someone with a lot of money, someone with pets, someone looking for a place for his grandmother. Also ask students to explain how they decided which places were (not) suited to each person. Divide students into pairs to write an ad for their own house/apartment, using the ones in the book as models. Circulate to help with vocabulary and collect the ads after about 5 minutes. Tell students that they are looking for a new place to live, and select 5-7 of the ads they wrote to read aloud. Have students listen to and note some feature which would make them want or not want to live there. After reading the selected ads, call on students to find out which were the most/least appealing houses.

B. Entrevistas. Dividing students into pairs for short interviews gives individual students more time to practice speaking and listening. Distribute interview cards with the questions below to pairs of students, or write the questions on the board. Allow 2-3 minutes for students to interview each other, then call on several pairs to "perform" their interviews for the whole class.

Student 1 Ask your partner:
- where s/he puts his/her clothes
- what time s/he goes to bed
- when s/he eats lunch

Student 2 Ask your partner:
- what time s/he gets up
- if s/he sings while showering
- where s/he does his/her homework

C. Diálogos: En una fiesta. Divide the class into four groups. Tell students they are at a cocktail party and that they are to mingle with one other person from each group. They should use a different set of questions from the Student Supplement (p. 65) with each new person. Set a time limit of 2 minutes for each mingle session. Afterward, have several students talk about some of the people they've met.

D. Guided Writing: En casa de doña Lupe. See p. 55 of the Student Supplement for the picture and questions. Assign the guided writing for homework and the next day have ten students put their sentences on the board. Correct errors as a class and then have students prepare dialogues between any two characters in the drawing using Chapter 4 vocabulary. As a follow-up, have students write a 100-word letter from Rosalía to a friend in which she talks about her family and what she does on weekends.

CAPÍTULO 5

Communicative Goals for Chapter 5
By the end of the chapter students should be able to:

* talk about the weather	☐
* describe what you do seasonally	☐
* point out where things are located	☐
* talk about what they are doing right now	☐
* describe personality traits and conditions	☐
* make simple comparisons	☐

Grammatical Structures
Students should know:

* prepositions of place	☐
* present progressive	☐
* **ser** vs. **estar**	☐
* **más/menos . . . que**	☐
* **tan . . . como**	☐
* **tanto/a/os/as . . . como**	☐

I. PRONUNCIATION

A. As a warm-up activity, have students practice "r" sounds using vocabulary from Chapter 5. Say each word in each of the associated-word groups and have students repeat. Ask students to think of other words for each category.

primavera	marzo	abril	hacer fresco
estar alegre	llover	parque	afuera
verano	hacer calor	nadar	mar
celebrar	descansar	tomar el sol	regresar a casa
otoño	septiembre	octubre	noviembre
hacer frío	llover	estar nublado	hacer fresco
invierno	diciembre	enero	febrero
nevar	esquiar	patinar	hacer frío

B. For more practice with r and rr, have students repeat the proverbs on p. 69 of the Student Supplement.

II. LISTENING COMPREHENSION

A. Weather Reports. Read the following weather reports to students as they complete the chart on p. 70 of the Student Supplement.

INSTRUCTIONS (read to students):

You will hear brief weather reports for five U.S. cities. As you listen, write the name of the city next to the picture that best matches its weather description. Then complete the chart by listening for the high and low temperatures for that city and the weather forecast for the next day. One picture will not be used. You will hear the reports twice.

- Buenos días, radiooyentes de Dallas. Ahora el boletín de las ocho. Otro día soleado aquí en Dallas, con temperaturas máximas alcanzando los 85 grados y las mínimas tal vez bajando hasta los 50 esta noche. Para mañana, se espera otro día muy agradable, despejado, con vientos leves del norte.

- Buenos días, Filadelfia. El Servicio Nacional Climatológico les trae las últimas noticias sobre la primera tempestad del invierno. Está nevando fuertemente ahora, con acumulaciones en algunas partes de Filadelfia de hasta 14 pulgadas, con temperaturas máximas sólo alcanzando los 35 grados. Esta noche, se espera temperaturas bajando hasta los 15 grados. Por suerte, mañana va a dejar de nevar. Va a hacer sol, pero continuará el frío intenso.

- Buenos días, Miami. Les traigo el boletín del mediodía. No salgan hoy sin impermeable, porque se esperan lluvias torrenciales para hoy, continuando por la tarde. El frente tropical llegó, y ya está lloviendo a cántaros en algunas partes de Miami. Debido a las lluvias, la temperatura ha bajado desde un alto de 92 grados hasta la temperatura mínima actual de 74 grados. Para mañana, se espera otra vez lluvia y muchísima humedad.

- Buenas tardes, Los Ángeles. El Servicio Nacional Climatológico advierte que, otra vez, los niveles de smog han alcanzado niveles peligrosos. Hoy se espera que el tiempo va a seguir igual que ayer, nublado, con temperaturas máximas llegando tal vez a los 65 grados y las mínimas bajando hasta los 50. Para mañana, se espera un día de sol con una leve subida de temperatura.

- Buenas tardes, Chicago. Aquí en la Ciudad Ventosa se espera un día típico de invierno, con un viento fuertísimo del Lago Michigan y un frío intensísimo. Se espera que la temperatura máxima alcanzará los 26 grados, con temperaturas mínimas bajando a los 12 grados esta noche. Mañana va a estar nublado, con posibilidades de nieve por la tarde y la noche.

B. Un poco de geografía. Have students refer to the maps on p. 71 of the Student Supplement while you read true/false geography statements to them.

¿Cierto o falso?

1. México está al este de Panamá.
2. Caracas está muy cerca de Santiago.
3. Bolivia está al lado del Perú.
4. La Argentina está al sur de Brasil.
5. El Perú está al oeste de Brasil.
6. Cuba está al oeste de Puerto Rico.
7. Caracas está al sur de Buenos Aires.
8. Nicaragua está entre Costa Rica y Honduras.
9. Panamá está al norte de Venezuela.
10. La República Dominicana está al oeste de Cuba.

Preguntas

You may want students to continue referring to the maps for these short-answer geography questions.

1. ¿Dónde está la República Dominicana?
2. ¿Cuál es la capital de Paraguay?
3. ¿Dónde está el Canal de Panamá?
4. ¿Cuál es la capital de Uruguay?
5. ¿Es Paraguay una isla?
6. ¿Dónde está el Mar Caribe?
7. ¿Cuál es la capital del Perú?
8. ¿Guatemala está cerca de Bolivia?
9. ¿Cuál es la capital de Costa Rica?
10. ¿Dónde está Colombia?
11. ¿Cuál es el país de habla española más grande de Sudamérica?
12. ¿Cuál es el país más grande de América Central?
13. ¿Qué países están cerca de la Argentina?
14. ¿Qué países están cerca de Nicaragua?

C. Preguntas personales. Use these questions for warm-up, as the basis of class discussions, or for daily practice.

1. ¿Cuál es tu estación favorita? ¿Por qué?
2. ¿Qué te gusta hacer cuando hace sol? ¿Y cuando llueve?
3. ¿Cuándo es tu cumpleaños?
4. ¿Cuál es tu clase más difícil?
5. ¿Qué haces cuando estás nervioso/a?
6. Por lo general, ¿tu cuarto está desordenado o limpio?
7. ¿Cuál es peor, estar aburrido o estar preocupado? ¿Por qué?
8. ¿Estudias más o menos que tu mejor amigo/a?
9. ¿Cuál es más importante, la clase de español o la clase de __________?
10. ¿Eres más o menos extrovertido/a que tu mejor amigo/a?
11. ¿Eres más o menos alto/a que tu madre/padre?
12. ¿Quién tiene más trabajo que yo?
13. ¿Piensas que los republicanos son mejores que los demócratas?
14. ¿Qué estás haciendo en este momento?
15. ¿Qué estoy haciendo yo?

D. ¿Quién es? (Drawing in Student Supplement, p. 72) This is a fun listening comprehension activity which practices with the prepositions **encima de, a la izquierda de**, etc. Read to the class the descriptions of the people and their locations in relation to one another. Students listen and fill in the information on the drawings in their Supplements. This can be done as a pop quiz or class activity.

1. Hay una sola persona aquí que lleva sombrero. Se llama Raúl.
2. Raúl está a la derecha del estudiante punky, Animal. Animal tiene pelo corto y lleva una cosa en la oreja.
3. Paco es estudiante en la universidad. Ahora está feliz porque sacó una nota muy alta en su examen de español.
4. Encima de Paco hay un perro muy lindo. El perro se llama Killer.

5. A la derecha de Killer está Juanito. Hoy Juanito está triste y cansado. Tiene pelo largo.
6. Debajo de Juanito hay una mujer embarazada. Está sentada y está pensando en el bebé. Ella se llama Gloria.
7. A la izquierda de Gloria está Paco, pero a la derecha de ella hay otra mujer muy guapa que lleva una ensalada de fruta encima de la cabeza. Se llama Carmen.
8. Encima de Carmen hay una estudiante muy trabajadora que está leyendo su libro de texto para la clase de español. Se llama Bárbara.
9. A la izquierda de Animal y encima de Killer hay un estudiante. Ahora está nervioso porque tiene miedo de los exámenes de español. Se llama Biff.

III. GRAMMAR

The following worksheets are in the Student Supplement.

A. Present Progressive. (p. 73) This art-based practice works with progressive forms and introduces some **ser** vs. **estar** contrast.

B. ¿Ser o estar? (p. 74) This list of English sentences helps students distinguish between the uses of the two verbs. A good first-day activity.

C. ¿Ser o estar? Párrafo. (p. 75) A cloze passage incorporating most of the uses of the two verbs.

D. Verbos: Ser vs. Estar. (p. 76) A multiple-choice worksheet.

E. Las comparaciones. (p. 77) A two-part worksheet practicing with comparisons of adjectives, verbs, and adverbs.

F. Repaso. (pages 78-81)

IV. INTEGRATIVE ACTIVITIES

A. Entrevistas: ¿Cómo estás? (p. 82) This is an interview-type activity which practices with the use of **estar** and conditions (**estoy triste, furioso, cansado,** etc.). An interview sheet is included in the Student Supplement; you may wish to amplify the questions with these or other additional ones.

1. Cuando tienes una cita con el hombre/la mujer ideal, ¿cómo estás?
2. Cuando es domingo por la noche y todavía necesitas hacer tu tarea para todas tus clases, cómo estás?
3. Cuando tienes un examen enorme, ¿cómo estás?
4. Cuando tus amigos te invitan a una fiesta, ¿cómo estás?
5. Cuando no entiendes tu tarea de español, ¿cómo estás?
6. Cuando un amigo te llama por teléfono mientras estás viendo tu programa de televisión favorito, ¿cómo estás?
7. Cuando no tienes planes para el fin de semana, ¿cómo estás?

B. Diálogos: Capítulo 5. (p. 83) As always, call on several pairs to perform their dialogues for the class. After the presentations, spend some time reviewing common errors.

C. Guided Writing: En la residencia. See p. 84 of the Student Supplement for picture and accompanying questions. Follow up by having students put their sentences on the board for class review and by having students prepare short dialogues between two of the people pictured in the drawing. As a final exercise, have the class write a 100-word letter from one of the students in the drawing to a family member back home. In their letters, they should include Chapter 5 vocabulary and structures.

D. Picture description. This activity is a good practice for **ser/estar** and comparisons. Bring in three pictures of interesting-looking people, large enough so the class can see them from the board. Tape the pictures to the board. In pairs, have students prepare the following information using the pictures and their imaginations:

1. Identificación **(¿Quién es?)**
2. Nacionalidad **(¿De dónde es?)**
3. Personalidad **(¿Cómo es?)**
4. Ubicación **(¿Dónde está?)**
5. Condición en este momento **(¿Cómo está?)**

Then, have students compare the three people. Ask pairs to write three comparative statements, one with adjectives, one with nouns, and one irregular comparison. You may give them a list of words to use in their comparisons (**interesante, inteligente, dinero, trabajar**, etc.), or you might model some sentences with the class.

V. GAMES

A. Password. Password works well for this chapter since there is so much concrete vocabulary. You may want to model some definitions for your students: **El mes entre marzo y mayo**; **Lo opuesto de triste**, etc.

CAPÍTULO 6

Communicative Goals for Chapter 6
By the end of the chapter students should be able to:

* discuss what they eat and drink ☐
* describe their favorite restaurant ☐
* order and pay for food ☐
* talk about what and who they know ☐
* answer questions negatively ☐
* tell someone to do something ☐

Grammatical Structures
Students should know:

* **saber y conocer** ☐
* personal **a** ☐
* direct object pronouns ☐
* **acabar de** ☐
* indefinite & negative words ☐
* formal commands ☐

I. PRONUNCIATION

A. Review the Spanish vowel sounds using the pronunciation practice sheet on p. 85 of the Student Supplement. Ask students to think of other food-related words for each vowel.

B. Dichos. Your students may also enjoy practicing new food vocabulary with these Spanish proverbs. Put these up on a transparency or give copies to students and have them repeat after you.

Quien come la carne, que roa el hueso.
Cena poco, come más y vivirás.
No comas crudo, ni andes el pie desnudo.
Quien come y deja, dos veces pone mesa.
Quien viejo engorda, dos mocedades goza.
Aceituna, una, y si es buena, una docena.
Carne de pluma quita del rostro la arruga.
La olla sin cebolla, es boda sin tamborín.
Con pan y vino se anda el camino.
Al pan, pan y al vino, vino.

II. LISTENING COMPREHENSION

A. Definiciones. Use statements like these for daily listening comprehension practice, for pop quizzes, or for vocabulary review. These definitions can be turned into true/false statements by including the correct or incorrect word in the definition: "La leche es una bebida alcohólica."

1. Una bebida de frutas o verduras.
2. Se usa para preparar sándwiches.
3. La comida favorita de los ratones.
4. La comida que se come por la mañana.
5. La bebida tradicional de los americanos.
6. Un ingrediente importante de un omelet.
7. Las manzanas, las bananas y las naranjas.
8. Una bebida que uno toma con el desayuno.
9. La comida que se come al mediodía (*noon*).
10. Una bebida alcohólica de color blanco o tinto.
11. Una sopa que uno toma cuando está enfermo.
12. Una comida muy común en la China y el Japón.
13. El plato que se come después del plato principal.

14. El plato líquido que se come con cuchara (*spoon*).
15. Una bebida que uno toma cuando tiene mucha sed.
16. Un postre que se sirve en las fiestas de cumpleaños.
17. Una verdura frita que se come con las hamburguesas.
18. La carne tradicional para las barbacoas en los Estados Unidos.
19. Un plato que se come antes del plato principal.
20. Los camarones y la langosta.
21. El jamón, el bistec y el pollo.
22. Un postre típico de España.
23. Un plato típico de México.
24. Una verdura anaranjada.
25. Una fruta amarilla.
26. Una verdura verde.
27. Un postre muy frío.
28. Una fruta roja.

B. Una noche en el Restaurante Monterrey. Students listen to the description of the activities in the restaurant while looking at the picture on p. 86 of the Student Supplement and then answer the true/false questions below the picture. The first time you read the passage, have students identify the people described by writing their names of the drawing. The second time, have students listen for the answers to the true/false questions.

Esta noche hay mucha gente en el Restaurante Monterrey. Por ejemplo, la familia Gómez está allí, celebrando el cumpleaños de la abuela. ¡Ayer ella cumplió 90 años! Cerca de la familia Gómez están sentados el Sr. y la Sra. Pañas. Son recién casados, y están viajando por España para su luna de miel. Salieron de la Argentina la semana pasada y van a pasar dos semanas en Europa. El Sr. Peñas está pidiendo la especialidad de la casa; la Sra. Peñas va a pedir un filete para su cena. En este momento, José y su amiga Beatriz están entrando al restaurante. José es muy cortés y ayuda a Beatriz a quitarse el abrigo. Ellos tienen una mesa reservada para las 8. Los dos están nerviosos porque es su primera cita. Cerca de la cocina está Marisa con su esposo Jean-Paul. Jean-Paul es francés y es muy delicado con lo que come y bebe. Ahora mismo, los dos están probando un vino tinto español para ver si está bien. Cerca de la entrada, el Sr. López paga la cuenta. Él cena en un restaurante diferente prácticamente todas las noches porque es soltero y no le gusta cocinar. La dependienta con quien habla el Sr. López está muy contenta porque él acaba de darle una propina muy grande.

¿Cierto o falso?

1. José and Beatriz will probably sit down next to the Gómez family.
2. Jean-Paul, when visiting the U.S., likes to eat in Arby's and Taco Bell.
3. The Gómez family is celebrating Mr. Gómez's birthday.
4. Sr. López eats in the Monterrey very frequently.
5. Sr. Peñas is ordering for himself and his wife.
6. The cashier is smiling because she's in love with Sr. López.
7. José has good manners.
8. The newlyweds are returning home in two days.

C. Preguntas. Use questions like these as part of warm-up or as the basis for class discussion.

1. ¿Cuál es tu comida favorita?
2. ¿Quién es vegetariano/a en esta clase?
3. ¿Quién desayuna? ¿Quién no?
4. ¿Cuál es la comida más importante para ti?
5. ¿Cuál es un/a desayuno/almuerzo/cena típico/a para ti?
6. ¿Cocinas bien? ¿Qué platos sabes preparar?
7. Cuando un amigo cena en tu casa, ¿qué le preparas?
8. ¿Cuál es tu postre favorito?
9. ¿Adónde vas cuando quieres comer algo rico pero malo para la salud?
10. ¿Quién está a dieta? ¿Qué cosas puedes comer? ¿Qué cosas no debes comer?
11. ¿A qué hora tienes hambre, generalmente?
12. En tu opinión, ¿dónde sirven las mejores papas fritas? ¿Y los mejores tacos?
13. ¿Qué restaurantes recomiendas para una cita romántica? ¿Para comer bien pero barato?
14. ¿Qué platos debemos preparar para nuestra fiesta al final del semestre?

III. GRAMMAR

The following worksheets are included in the Student Supplement.

A. Saber vs. conocer worksheet. (p. 88) For additional practice, have students translate the sentences in Part I.

B. Saber vs. conocer. (p. 89) A cloze passage.

C. Direct Object Pronouns. (p. 90) You can assign these questions as homework and have students use them in pair interviews the next day. For more practice with direct object pronouns, see the suggestion below, as well as the pronoun game suggested in the "Games" sections of the Chapter 6 Teacher's Guide.

If students are having trouble understanding how direct object pronouns work, try this presentation. Put the text and the picture below up on a transparency. Read the description aloud, asking students to explain to what or to whom the direct object pronouns in boldface refer. As students answer, use the transparency picture to draw arrows to the nouns replaced by pronouns.

Esta noche, los Sres. Nieto invitan a los García a comer. **Los** invitan porque es el cumpleaños del Sr. Nieto. Los niños están arriba en la alcoba y hacen mucho ruido, pero los padres no **los** oyen porque están en la sala, escuchando la radio. **La** están escuchando porque hay un programa muy interesante a las 6:30. Todos quieren escuchar**lo**, porque habla de la música tejana. A las 6:45 suena el teléfono, pero no **lo** oyen tampoco.

Después de escuchar el programa, van a comer hamburguesas en el patio. A todos les gustan las hamburguesas de la Sra. Nieto. ¡El perro quiere comer**las** ahora mismo! El perro está en el patio en este momento, pero nadie **lo** ve porque la puerta está cerrada. A las 7:15 van a llamar a los niños a comer. No van a llamar**los** antes, porque prefieren hablar un rato sin interrupciones.

D. ¿Qué acaban de hacer y qué van a hacer? (p. 91) An art-based worksheet practicing with these two constructions.

E. Indefinite and negative words. (p. 92) This art-based practice contrasts these words in an opposition format.

F. Mandatos formales. (p. 93) An advice-giving activity.

G. Traducciones: Mandatos formales. (p. 94) Practices with **Ud./Uds**. commands and object pronouns.

H. Práctica: Mandatos formales. (pages 95-96) Students may find filling in the charts helpful for memorizing forms and placement of object pronouns.

I. Repaso: Capítulo 6. (pages 97-99)

For extra grammar practice and review, some teachers find it helpful to gather common student errors and distribute them to the class for correction. Here are some errors to use for Chapter 6. You can put these on a transparency for a group proofreading session, or photocopy them.

1. No conozco el número de teléfono del profesor.
2. No sé Juan muy bien.
3. Espero al autobús.
4. Espero María.
5. Ningunos estudiantes llegan tarde.
6. ¡Estás en clase nunca!
7. ¡Quiero no estudiar!
8. No hay alguna película buena este fin de semana.
9. ¿Vas a invitar alguien?
10. No llamo nadie.
11. No salgo con alguien este fin de semana.
12. Estudio nunca el viernes por la noche.
13. ¿Conoces mi amigo?

IV. INTEGRATIVE ACTIVITIES

A. "En la Hostería del Laurel." Doing restaurant-scene skits is a fun activity. First, read as a class the dialogue on p. 205 of *Puntos*, or watch the corresponding video episode. Put some useful restaurante phrases on the board or a transparency (**Me trae un/una __________, por favor; ¿Qué desean Uds. de plato principal/postre/etcétera?; ¿Algo más?**; and so forth) and review with students. Then go over the menu from the Spanish restaurant on p. 87 of the Student Supplement. Ask students to use their imaginations to describe what the following dishes consist of: **Urta roteña, pollo sevillano, sopa de picadillo**, and **postre Hostería**. Bring in a tablecloth and some plastic plates and utensils and set up a corner of the room as a restaurant. Then assign roles to three students (waiter and diners) and let them go through the process of entering a restaurant, ordering a meal, and paying. The clients should ask the waiter to describe some dishes on the menu and to make some recommendations. Encourage students to use all possible expressions. This is an activity that can be repeated over two or three days. As always, follow up by clarifying problems and pointing out common errors.

B. <u>Entrevista: La comida y los gustos</u>. Have students in pairs interview each other using the questions on p. 100 of the Student Supplement. After the interviews, ask questions about which students like/dislike certain foods, and try to come to a consensus about the class' most/least favorite foods.

C. <u>La fiesta de la clase de español</u>. Divide the class into groups of 4-5 students, and ask them to work out all of the details of the end-of-semester class party to present to the rest of the class. Each group member will have a different detail or details:

- what food to serve
- whom they will invite
- who will bring the music
- where the party will be and when
- who will help organize and clean up
- who will bring things to drink
- what sort of entertainment they will have

Give individual members 2-3 minutes to arrange their details, then give the whole group another 3-4 minutes to organize the party plan. Have one or more members from each group explain their plans for the party to the rest of the class, and have the class vote on the best/worst party, best food suggestions, etc.

D. <u>Guided Writing: En la cafetería universitaria</u>. See p. 102 of the Student Supplement for picture and accompanying questions. It is very helpful to have students put their answers on the board. Students can work in pairs to figure out which sentences contain errors. An excellent follow-up is to have students prepare short, spontaneous dialogues between any two characters in the drawing. Encourage them to use the new vocabulary from Chapter 6. You might also have students write a 100-word letter from one of the people in the drawing to a friend or relative, again using Chapter 6 vocabulary and structures.

E. <u>Communicative Goals Practice #2</u>. See p. 103 of the Student Supplement for the picture and instructions for the student. This speaking practice is excellent preparation for the final oral interviews and a good way of practice the communicative goals in a global way. For more ideas on using these practices, see the "Integrative Activities" section of the Chapter 2 Teacher's Guide, p. 16

V. GAMES

A. Bingo: Capítulo 6. See p. 101 of the Student Supplement for a food bingo.

B. Password. Password works especially will for Chapter 6 since there is so much concrete vocabulary.

C. Direct-object game. Have students write 2-3 sentences, each containing a direct object. Tell them to rewrite the sentences, substituting the correct direct object pronoun (e.g., **Nunca preparo el desayuno ⇒ Nunca lo preparo.)** Check over the sentences and the rewrites (you may want to do this a day before the game). Then break up the class into 2 teams. A student from Team A reads a sentence to a student from Team B. The student from Team B must rephrase the sentence, substituting the direct object with the correct direct-object pronoun. If s/he does so successfully, Team B wins a point and so on. A more sophisticated version of this game is for students to write questions which use a direct object pronoun in the answer: **¿Tienes que preparar la cena esta noche? Sí, la tengo que preparar.** The rules are the same; again, you may want to have students do the preliminary writing the day before.

CAPÍTULO 7

Communicative Goals for Chapter 7
By the end of the chapter students should be able to:

* talk about trips and traveling	☐
* express to whom and for whom they do something	☐
* talk about likes and dislikes more fully	☐
* talk about things that happened in the past	☐

Grammatical Structures
Students should know:

* indirect object pronouns	☐
* **dar** and **decir**	☐
* **gustar**	☐
* preterite forms	☐
* uses of the preterite	☐

I. PRONUNCIATION

A. The following sentences contain some sounds difficult for students: **r**, **j**, **x**, initial **p**, silent **h**, and intervocalic **s**. Use them to build word-chains for students to practice and repeat. Read the sentences in the chunks indicated until students are saying the whole sentence, while they follow on p. 105 of the Student Supplement. Then have students work in pairs to practice these 5 sentences.

1. No hay ningún asiento

   en el autobús

   No hay ningún asiento en el autobús

   que va al aeropuerto.

   No hay ningún asiento / en el autobús / que va al aeropuerto.

2. En el Hotel Majestad / el maletero nos ayuda / con un montón de maletas.
3. El piloto le pregunta / al pasajero puertorriqueño / si va a Pamplona o Pontevedra.
4. Recibimos tarjetas postales / de Cancún, Oaxaca, / Guanajuato e Isla Mujeres.
5. Guárdame un asiento / en el siguiente vuelo / a Uruguay. / ¡Es urgente!

B. For more practice with the **g**, **gu**, and **j** sounds, have students repeat the proverbs on p. 105 of the Student Supplement.

II. LISTENING COMPREHENSION

A. Definiciones/Cierto-Falso. These statements can be used for daily listening comprehension practice, vocabulary review, or pop quizzes. They may be converted into true/false statements by including the correct/incorrect definitions: **La persona que lleva las maletas es la azafata.**

1. La persona que lleva las maletas de los pasajeros.
2. El tipo de billete que compras si vas a salir de y regresar al mismo lugar.
3. El lugar donde hay muchos trenes y/o autobuses.
4. El lugar donde hay muchos aviones.

5. El modo de transporte que debes usar si te gusta mucho el agua.
6. El papel que necesitas comprar antes de hacer un viaje.
7. Lo opuesto de la salida.
8. Lo opuesto de llegar a tiempo.
9. La persona que trabaja para una línea aérea y que ayuda a los pasajeros en los aviones.
10. Un término general para las maletas, las bolsas, etc.
11. El lugar en un aeropuerto donde los viajeros duermen, fuman, leen, etc.
12. Lo opuesto de subir al avión.
13. Si no tienes el dinero para viajar en primera clase, debes viajar en _________.
14. Una actividad muy aburrida que tienes que hacer en los aeropuertos y el banco.
15. El lugar que ocupas durante el vuelo.
16. El documento oficial que necesitas para viajar al extranjero.
17. Un tipo de coche muy grande.
18. Lo que necesitas si vas a hacer camping.

B. Multiple Choice. Again, these statements are good for practice or pop quizzes.

1. Si no tienes mucho dinero, necesitas comprar: a) un boleto de clase turística, b) un boleto de primera clase, c) un pasaje de primera clase en el barco "Reina Isabel II".
2. Vas a ir a Miami en avión, pero piensas volver en coche. Necesitas: a) un boleto de ida y vuelta, b) un boleto de ida sólo, c) dos boletos de primera clase.
3. Si un avión debe salir a las 8:00, pero no sale hasta las 8:45, es porque: a) hay dos escalas, b) el piloto quiere llegar a tiempo, c) hay una demora.
4. Si no te gustan los cigarrillos, pides un asiento en: a) la sección de fumar, b) primera clase, c) la sección de no fumar.
5. No te gustan los aviones. ¿Cómo puedes viajar rápidamente desde Orlando a Washington D.C.? a) en bicicleta, b) en tren, c) en barco.
6. Si tienes que llegar a Nueva York muy pronto, necesitas un vuelo: a) sin escalas, b) atrasado, c) con muchas escalas.
7. ¿Qué debes hacer si tienes mucho equipaje? a) llevarlo contigo en el avión, b) facturarlo, c) dejarlo en la sala de espera.
8. Antes de ir de viaje, necesitas: a) hacer una escala, b) hacer la maleta, c) hacer camping.
9. El lugar donde compras los boletos de avión es: a) la agencia de viajes, b) la sala de espera, c) la estación del tren.
10. Si tienes un montón de dinero y quieres hacer un viaje de lujo desde Nueva York a Madrid, puedes pedir: a) un boleto de tren, b) un boleto de avión de clase turística, c) una cabina en un barco grande y elegante.

C. Jaime y Marta se van de viaje. This listening comprehension activity practices with the new preterite forms, as well as Chapter 7 vocabulary. Read students the script as they complete the chart on p. 107 of the Student Supplement.

INSTRUCTIONS: You will hear a short conversation between Jaime and Marta, who are getting ready for a trip. As you listen, indicate what they have already done to get ready and what they still need to do in the chart below. Place an X in the correct column, based on what you hear. Look over the list of actions before you begin.

Marta: Mi amor, ¿dónde están las maletas? No las encuentro en el garaje.
Jaime: Ya las busqué. Las saqué del garaje ayer y las puse en nuestra alcoba. ¿Cuándo vamos a hacer las maletas?
Marta: Pues, creo que debemos hacerlas mañana, ¿no?
Jaime: De acuerdo. Oye, y ya encontré nuestros pasaportes--estaban en el escritorio de la sala.
Marta: Muy bien. Pues, llamé esta mañana a la línea aérea y nos confirmé el vuelo, pero todavía necesitamos hacer las reservaciones del hotel.
Jaime: ¿Hablaste con la agente de viajes?
Marta: No, la voy a llamar ahora. Creo que voy a pasar por la agencia esta tarde, porque también tengo que ir al banco y comprarnos unos cheques de viajero. Y—¡ay!—casi se me olvida...todavía hay que comprar los boletos, ¿verdad?
Jaime: Tranquila, mi amor. ¿No te acuerdas que te dije que compré los boletos ayer, cuando estaba en el centro? Están con nuestros pasaportes, en la sala.
Marta: Ah, sí, ahora me acuerdo. Pues, creo que voy a salir ahora para hacer estas cosas.
Jaime: Bueno, cuando salgas, ¿puedes comprar película para la cámara? No tuve tiempo de hacerlo ayer.
Marta: No te preocupes, mi amor. Compré 6 rollos de película esta mañana cuando fui al supermercado.
Jaime: Ah, perfecto. Entonces, ¿qué más tenemos que hacer?
Marta: ¿Por qué no hacemos una lista ahora mismo? Así no se nos olvida nada.
Jaime: ¡Buena idea!

D. Discrimination practice: ¿Presente o pretérito? After presenting the preterite material on pages 234-235 of *Puntos*, read sentences like those below to your students. The first time you read, ask students to write "Present" or "Past" according to what they hear. Then read the sentences again and ask students to identify the subject. Don't read all these sentences at once; do them in batches of 8-10 over a couple of days. This practice is a good warm-up activity.

Recibe buenas notas siempre.
Vivió en Caracas por 3 años.
Es una persona fenomenal.
Habló con su mamá por teléfono.
Vende ropa barata en el mercado.
Aprendiste los verbos, ¿verdad?
¿Qué hizo Juan con el dinero?
No comprendo el problema
Aprendió francés en Canadá.
Tomas una clase de química, ¿no?
Teresa no contestó el teléfono.
¿Compraste la blusa o la camiseta?

Dio una fiesta.
Sale a las dos.
¿Hiciste tu tarea?
Estudia conmigo.
Fui al cine con Luis.
Escuchó el nuevo disco.
Me levanté a las ocho.
Bebí un vaso de agua.
Hice algo estúpido ayer.
Recibió una carta ayer.
Tomé el examen a las tres.
Marcos sale con Lupe el viernes.

E. Preguntas personales. Use questions like these for warm-up, daily listening comprehension practice, or as the basis of a class discussion.

1. ¿Te gusta viajar? ¿Adónde vas a ir para las vacaciones de Navidad/de primavera?
2. ¿Te gusta viajar por avión o tienes miedo?
3. En general, ¿cómo prefieres viajar? ¿Por qué?
4. ¿Cómo pasas el tiempo cuando viajas?
5. ¿Cuál fue tu mejor viaje?
6. Cuando viajas, ¿les escribes tarjetas postales a tus amigos?
7. Cuando haces un viaje a México, ¿les compras recuerdos a tus padres?
8. ¿Adónde te gustaría viajar en el futuro?
9. ¿Adónde te gustaría viajar para tu luna de miel?
10. ¿Dónde te gustaría vivir después de graduarte?
11. ¿Cuáles son dos cosas que no te gustan? ¿Y dos cosas que te gustan muchísimo?
12. ¿Qué le gusta hacer a tu madre? ¿a tu padre? ¿a tu mejor amigo/a?

F. Dictado. Have one student write the sentences at the board as you dictate to the whole class. Speak at a close to natural speed and break the sentences up according to the slashes below. Read each sentence once, then tell students how many words are in the sentence, then repeat. Review each sentence with the class.

1. Para mis próximas vacaciones / me gustaría ir a algún lugar / con muchas playas / y poca gente. (16)
2. Cuando mi mamá viaja por avión / siempre toma tres copas de vino / porque tiene mucho miedo. (16)
3. No me gusta facturar mi equipaje / porque pienso que las líneas aéreas / van a perder mis maletas. (17)
4. El próximo verano, / Jaime y Dolores van a hacer un viaje / desde la Florida hasta Colorado / en bicicleta. (18)
5. En el futuro, me gustaría hacer / un viaje en un barco crucero / y viajar con todo lujo. (16)

G. "En el aeropuerto." This is an airport scene in which students identify the people you describe. The script is below; the picture is in the Student Supplement, p. 106. This script can be re-used the next day as a dictation exercise.

INSTRUCTIONS: Tell students to write down the name of the person being described.

Hay mucha gente en Barajas, el aeropuerto de Madrid. Roberto trabaja allí y en este momento está poniendo la hora de llegada de los vuelos que llegan por la tarde. Marco tiene mucho equipaje. Le da algún dinero al maletero porque lo ayudó con sus tres maletas. ¡Pobre Fred! Está muy confundido. No lee español y está entrando en los servicios para mujeres. José no sabe a qué hora despega su avión para Barcelona. Por eso le está pidiendo información a la señorita. Juanita acaba de llegar con su hijo Ramón. Los dos están buscando a la hermana de Juanita. Ramón acaba de ver a su tía y ahora está saludándola. Margarita está facturando su equipaje. Está contenta porque no tiene que hacer cola. Luis y Elena están enamorados. No quieren separarse, pero Luis tiene que ir a Francia y Elena se queda en Madrid.

III. GRAMMAR

The following worksheets are in the Student Supplement.

A. Indirect object pronouns. (p. 108) This two-part practice works with the new pronouns, as well as verbs that commonly take indirect objects.

B. Direct vs. Indirect object pronouns. (p. 109) A good discrimination worksheet.

C. Preguntas personales. (p. 110) These questions elicit both kinds of object pronouns in the responses. This worksheet also helps students distinguish between the two kinds of pronouns.

D. Gustar. (p. 111) This two-part worksheet practices with **gustar** and similar verbs.

E. El pretérito. (p. 112)

F. Spelling changes in the preterite. (p. 113)

G. El pretérito: Práctica. (p. 114)

H. El pretérito: un asesinato. (p. 115) This two-page worksheet contains three linked cloze passages. Each passage is a statement from a person at the scene of a murder. As students complete the passages with the missing preterite forms, they are asked to find the person who lies in his/her statement. (HINT: Re-read doña Catalina's statement carefully.)

I. Repaso. (pp. 117-118)

IV. INTEGRATIVE ACTIVITIES

A. Entrevistas: "Mi próximo viaje". In this activity, students interview each other about upcoming trips. Begin by telling the class about your next trip, using **Quiero ir a..., Me gustaría ver..., Voy a...,** and so forth. Then ask the class to brainstorm questions they would use to ask someone about travel plans. Write them on the board and encourage students to think of follow-up questions. After you've established this interview question bank, divide the class into pairs. Give the pairs 3-4 minutes to interview each other using the questions the class has thought of, then call on a few pairs to either perform their interviews for the class or to tell the class about their partner's next trip.

B. Más entrevistas. This interview activity is more structured than the one above. Divide the class into pairs and distribute interview cards with the questions below to each pair of students, or write the questions on the board. Allow 2-3 minutes for students to interview each other and then have several pairs perform their interviews for the class.

Student 1 Ask your partner:
- what he/she likes to do after class
- where he/she went last year for vacation
- who helps him/her study Spanish

Student 2 Ask your partner:
- what he/she likes to eat at 11 p.m.
- what he/she did today before class
- if he/she can lend you $10.00

C. Charla: los estereotipos y el turismo. Begin this discussion by presenting the "typical" U.S. tourist. Give him/her a funny name and if possible, bring in a magazine picture that portrays this imaginary person. Ask the class for some stereotypes about U.S. tourists, and list their responses on the board. You can bring up topics like clothing, origin, language abilities, manners, cultural sensitivity, etc. Ask students if this sort of tourist really exists, if they know people like this, if all U.S. tourists are the same, etc. Then, after the class has identified the stereotypes, ask them for some ways to combat them. Tell students that the tourist whom you presented at the beginning of the discussion is planning yet another trip. What advice can students give this person to avoid some of the problems and mishaps of previous trips? Have students come up with a list of Dos and Don'ts using formal commands. List the suggestions on the board next to the stereotypes.

D. Diálogos: Capítulo 7. There are some good possibilities for dialogues on p. 240 of *Puntos*. Prepare for this activity by discussing the dialogue on p. 239 beforehand and doing some modeling with a few students. Give students 3-4 minutes to create their dialogues, and call on several pairs to present them to the class. Ask the class some simple comprehension questions following each of the dialogues. After all the presentations, review some common errors.

E. Guided Writing: En el aeropuerto de San José. See p. 119 of the Student Supplement for the picture and accompanying questions. Have students put the answers on the board. Use this opportunity to catch persistent errors. As a follow-up, have students prepare short, spontaneous dialogues between any two characters in the drawing or write a 100-word letter from one of the characters in the drawing to a friend or relative, discussing their trip.

V. GAMES

A. Hablando de gustos. See p. 120 of the Student Supplement for the form that students will complete in this information-gap activity. Model a sample question with students first, then set a time limit for students to find classmates who fit the various categories. Call on students who finish first to report their classmates' likes/dislikes to the class.

NOTE: If you didn't get around to playing "Gustar" bingo in Chapter 1, see p. 19 of the Student Supplement for the BINGO card. This game is great practice with **gustar**, especially when the winner reports on his/her answers.

B. Busca a alguien que... This poll-type game practices with the new preterite forms. See p. 121 of the Student Supplement for the poll.

CAPÍTULO 8

Communicative Goals for Chapter 8
By the end of the chapter students should be able to:

* discuss special holidays and parties ☐
* talk about how they feel in different situations ☐
* give empathetic opinions and reactions ☐
* talk more about past events ☐

Grammatical Structures
Students should know:

* **-ísimo/a** ☐
* irregular preterites ☐
* stem-changing preterites ☐
* double object pronouns ☐

I. PRONUNCIATION

Have students listen as you read this Christmas **villancico** from Argentina, then have them practice reading the text aloud with a partner. (Student Supplement, p. 123)

Los Reyes Magos

Llegaron ya los reyes
y eran tres,
Melchor, Gaspar
y el negro Baltazar.
Arrope y miel
le llevarán
y un poncho blanco
de alpaca real.

Changos y chinitas
duérmanse,
que ya Melchor,
Gaspar y Baltazar
todos los regalos
dejarán
para jugar mañana
el Redentor.

El niño Dios
muy bien lo agradeció;
comió la miel
y el poncho lo abrigó.
Y fue después
que los miró,
y a medianoche
el sol se alumbró.

II. LISTENING COMPREHENSION

A. Cierto/Falso. Give students 2 minutes to review the new vocabulary on p. 248 and 251 of their books, then read these **cierto/falso** statements.

1. El primero de enero es la Nochebuena.
2. Divertirse es un sinónimo de pasarlo bien.
3. Normalmente se celebra la Pascua en abril.
4. La última noche del año se llama la Navidad.
5. Celebramos el Día de Gracias en noviembre.
6. **Llorar** es un sinónimo de reírse.
7. Algo que alguien no sabe o que no espera es una sorpresa.
8. Si comes demasiados entremeses en una fiesta, te puedes enfermar.
9. Los padres se enojan cuando los hijos se portan bien.
10. Lo opuesto de recordar es olvidarse (de).

B. Dictado. Don't forget that dictations are excellent listening practice if the sentences are read in "chunks" of at least three words at a time. Have one student go to the side blackboard while the others do the dictation at their seats. Check each sentence right away. Read the sentence once as indicated, then tell them the number of words there are in the sentence and repeat it one more time.

1. ¿Cómo pasaste la Nochebuena / el año pasado? (7)

2. Tuve una invitación / de mis tíos / y fui a cenar con ellos. (12)
3. Ahora pónganse cómodos / y vamos a divertirnos. (7)
4. Como ya te dijimos / mañana vamos a estar aquí / a las nueve / para ayudarte a limpiar la casa. (18)

C. Listening Passage. Read the following passage twice to your students. The first time students should fill in the chart on p. 123 of the Student Supplement. The second time they put a ✓ next to the gifts from Los Reyes and an * next to the gifts from Santa Claus.

La madre de Carlos y Mónica es norteamericana; su padre es español. Por eso tienen la suerte de celebrar la Navidad dos veces cada año. Reciben regalos de Santa Claus la Nochebuena y regalos de los Reyes Magos el 6 de enero. Este año Carlos recibió una chaqueta negra y una bicicleta roja de Santa Claus y el 6 de enero recibió un acuario con muchos peces y una cámara de los Reyes. De Santa Claus, su hermana recibió un vestido rojo y 2 muñecas rubias con un cambio de ropa para cada una. Y de los Reyes, recibió un radio de color rosado y un gato gris.

D. Preguntas personales. These questions can be used as oral warm-up questions one day and as a dictation another. Sometimes writing the question, dictated in chunks, is a good way to get students to listen more carefully to the tense used in the question.

1. ¿Diste una fiesta el mes pasado?
2. ¿Faltaste a clase alguna vez esta semana?
3. ¿Qué le regalaste a tu mejor amigo/a para su cumpleaños?
4. ¿Te enojaste con alguien ayer? ¿Con quién y por qué?
5. ¿En qué situación te pones furioso/a?
6. ¿Dónde estuviste el Día de Gracias el año pasado?
7. ¿Cuándo viniste a la universidad hoy?
8. ¿Qué pediste la última vez que comiste en tu restaurante favorito?
9. ¿Cuántas horas dormiste anoche?
10. ¿Te divertiste la última vez que saliste con tus amigos?
11. ¿Cuál es el mejor restaurante de *(your town/city)*?
12. ¿Cuál fue la mejor película del año pasado?
13. ¿Cuál es el curso más difícil de esta universidad?
14. ¿Quién es la persona más importante de tu vida?

III. GRAMMAR

The following worksheets are in the Student Supplement.

A. Las emociones y las reacciones. (p. 124) A personalized worksheet practicing with the new vocabulary. This could be used for a pair interview.

B. Double object pronouns. (p. 125) An art-based practice related to Chapter 8 themes.

C. Sequence of object pronouns: Traducción. (p. 126) This translation drill is very helpful for practicing the new pronouns together.

D. El pretérito y los pronombres. (p. 127) These questions solicit preterite forms and double-object pronouns in the responses.

E. El pretérito. (p. 128) Three cloze passages, practicing with regular and irregular preterite forms.

F. Irregular and stem-changing preterites. (p. 130)

G. Práctica: Adjectives of emphasis. (p. 131) A three-part worksheet practicing the **-ísimo** forms.

H. Repaso. (pp. 132-134)

IV. INTEGRATIVE ACTIVITIES

A. Situaciones y diálogos. See p. 135 of the Student Supplement.

B. Guided Writing. See p. 137 of the Student Supplement for the picture and accompanying questions. Have students write their sentences on the board for class review, then have pairs of students present short dialogues between two of the people pictured in the drawing. As a final activity, have students write a 100-word letter from one of the guests pictured, describing the party.

V. GAMES

A. Verb competition. Divide the class into 2 teams. One member of each team goes to the board. You give an infinitive to these two students; they have to conjugate the verb in the preterite. The first one to write it correctly gets a point for their team.

venir	ellos	reírse	José
acostarse	Ud.	pedir	tú
preferir	nosotros	vestirse	Elisa y Elena
servir	María	sentirse	ella
dormir	Uds.	hacerse	tú
quejarse	yo	morirse	ellos
recordar	ella	sonreír	José y yo

B. Who did what? Have students write down just one sentence about what they did last Christmas or last Spring break, and collect them. The next day read the statements aloud in batches of five. Have students write the name of the classmate who they think corresponds to the statement. After reading the first group of five, see how many guessed correctly.

EXAMPLE: Compañero #1 fue a California para estar con su familia.
Compañero #2 pasó la Navidad en Acapulco.

C. Bingo. See p. 136 of the Student Supplement for the Chapter 8 Bingo card.

D. Double-Object Pronoun Game. Have each student write 2-3 sentences with both direct and indirect objects, and then have them rewrite the sentences, making the correct substitutions. To make the game more challenging, tell students that they need to use different pronouns and verbs in each sentence. Collect the sentences and look them over. The next day divide the class into two groups. Give one student from Team A a sentence to transform, and so on.

CAPÍTULO 9

Communicative Goals for Chapter 9
By the end of the chapter students should be able to:

- * talk about free time and household chores ☐
- * talk about what they used to do ☐
- * describe past conditions and states ☐
- * express extremes ☐

Grammatical Structures
Students should know:

- * imperfect of regular and irregular verbs ☐
- * superlatives ☐
- * question words ☐

I. PRONUNCIATION

Practice the **x**, **g**, and **j** sounds in these tongue-twisters: These sentences are in the Student Supplement at the top of p. 139.

- En México excelentes expertos mexicanos explican a excelentes expertos que para ser excelentes expertos no hay que ser excelentes expertos en México, sino excelentes expertos mexicanos en México.
- El gerente Gerardo Jiménez trabaja en una gestoría generalmente junto a jefes diligentes que generan urgentes gestiones.

II. LISTENING COMPREHENSION

A. ¿Qué pasa en la playa? This listening comprehension script practices with new chapter vocabulary. Have students look at the drawing and the questions at the bottom of p. 139 in the Student Supplement.

INSTRUCTIONS (read to students):

The first time you hear the description, write the names of the people mentioned on the drawing. The second time, listen for the answers to the questions below the drawing.

Hoy es el primero de julio, y se comienza la temporada de verano en la playa de Cádiz. Vamos a ver quiénes están en la playa hoy.

A Martín le encanta la natación, y es un nadador muy fuerte. El año pasado, participó en los Juegos Olímpicos. Guillermo y Lourdes vinieron a la playa para pasar su luna de miel. Ahora toman el sol y hacen planes para ir a un concierto de Carlos Cano esta noche.

A Inés le gusta el vólibol y es una jugadora excelente. Por desgracia, el año pasado no pudo jugar nada porque tuvo un accidente automovilístico. Pero ahora está fenomenal. De hecho, en este momento ella y su compañero Arturo les están ganando al otro equipo.

En este momento Rolando lo está pasando muy mal. Está preocupadísimo porque no sabe dónde está su hijita de dos años, y la está buscando en el mar. No sabe que su hija ya volvió al hotel con su mamá.

El Sr. Bravo es el tío de Nicolás y Clara. Vino a la playa hoy para cuidarlos. Pero es gran aficionado del fútbol, y ahora está leyendo el periódico para saber el resultado del partido Real Madrid-Betis. No ve que Nicolás y Clara ya corrieron para el otro lado de la playa.

1. ¿Qué le gusta hacer a Martín?
2. ¿Adónde van a ir Guillermo y Lourdes esta noche?
3. ¿Jugó Inés vólibol en año pasado? ¿Por qué?
4. ¿Por qué está preocupado Rolando?
5. ¿Qué debe hacer el Sr. Bravo en vez de leer el periódico?

B. Trabajando en casa. This listening comprehension script practices with household chores and recycles preterite. Have students look at the drawing and questions on p. 140 of the Student Supplement.

INSTRUCTIONS (read to students):

The first time you hear the description, identify the people below by writing each person's name next to him/her. Also listen for what chores each person has already done and what he/she still needs to do, and write them next to the appropriate person. The second time you hear the description, listen for the answers to the true-false statements below the drawing.

Los sábados casi siempre son días ocupados en casa de los Pacheco, porque hacen muchos quehaceres por la mañana. Todos ayudan en casa. Hoy, por ejemplo, el Sr. Pacheco está pasando la aspiradora. Está feliz ahora porque por fin terminó de sacudir todos los muebles de la sala -- ¡y el Sr. Pacheco odia sacudir los muebles porque es tan aburrido! Todavía necesita lavar el coche, pero eso no le va a llevar mucho tiempo, porque va a pedir la ayuda de sus hijos Iván y Lydia.

Al hijo Iván le toca lavar los platos ahora. No es una tarea muy difícil, ya que los Pacheco tienen lavaplatos. Iván ya sacó la basura de la cocina, pero todavía debe limpiar su cuarto. El cuarto de Iván siempre está muy desordenado, y él va a necesitar por lo menos una hora para limpiarlo y poner todo en su sitio. Lydia, la hermana de Miguel, ya limpió su cuarto e hizo su cama. Ella siempre hace esas cosas inmediatamente después de levantarse. Ahora a ella le toca lavar la ropa. Éste es otro quehacer bastante fácil, porque la lavadora y la secadora son nuevas y grandes. Sin embargo, Lydia todavía tiene que planchar toda la ropa después, y por eso no está muy contenta ahora. Tiene 5 camisas y 3 blusas para planchar, y unos pantalones y faldas también. Qué desagradable, ¿verdad?

¿Y la Sra. Pacheco? Ella típicamente ayuda en casa, pero ahora está haciendo la compra. Vienen unos invitados a cenar esta noche, y ella va a preparar la cena. Cuando regrese a casa, va a barrer el suelo del comedor y poner la mesa.

C. Preguntas personales. Use these as warm-up, discussion questions, or as a daily listening comprehension practice.

1. ¿Adónde vas para divertirte?
2. ¿Qué planes vas a hacer para el fin de semana?
3. ¿Es divertida o aburrida la clase de español?
4. ¿Cuál es la mejor discoteca de (*your town/city*)? ¿el mejor cine?
5. ¿Dónde hay un buen lugar para tomar el sol? ¿Para pasear en bicicleta? ¿Para nadar? ¿Hacer un *picnic*?
6. ¿Vas al cine con frecuencia? ¿Qué tipo de películas te gusta?
7. ¿Qué haces en tus ratos libres?

8. ¿Qué deportes practicas? ¿Cuánto tiempo hace que los practicas?
9. ¿Das muchas fiestas? ¿Cómo son tus fiestas?
10. ¿Prefieres practicar un deporte o ver un partido en la televisión?
11. ¿Te consideras una persona organizada/desorganizada?
12. Por lo general, ¿cómo está tu casa/apartamento, ordenada o desordenada?
13. ¿Cuántas horas pasas a la semana limpiando la casa?
14. Después de comer, ¿lavas los platos inmediatamente , o los dejas para el día siguiente?
15. Si tengo muchas cucarachas en mi cocina, ¿qué debo hacer?
16. ¿Qué hora era cuando te acostaste anoche?
17. ¿Cómo se llamaba tu escuela primaria?
18. ¿Qué programas de televisión veías con frecuencia cuando eras niño/a?
19. ¿Dónde vivías cuando tenías 10 años?
20. De niño/a, ¿caminabas a la escuela o tomabas el autobús?
21. ¿Te gustaba la comida picante cuando eras niño/a?

D. Definiciones. Use these definitions for daily listening comprehension practice, vocabulary review, pop quizzes, etc.

1. Si quieres tener un buen bronceado (*tan*), necesitas __________.
2. Un deporte muy popular en las montañas durante el invierno.
3. Lo opuesto de ganar.
4. Si alguien tiene mucho interés en un deporte, se dice que esa persona es __________.
5. Un deporte que se practica sobre el hielo.
6. Un deporte acuático.
7. El lugar adonde vas para bailar.
8. El lugar donde hay obras de arte, exposiciones, etc.
9. Un deporte muy popular en el mundo hispano, que se juega con una pelota blanca y negra.
10. El aparato que se usa para preparar algo de comer rápidamente.
11. El lugar donde se pone el helado, el hielo, etc.
12. Se hace cuando los muebles están sucios.
13. El aparato que usamos para limpiar el suelo o la alfombra.
14. El aparato que usamos para lavar la ropa.

E. Los pasatiempos favoritos de la clase de español. After presenting the chapter vocabulary, ask students to write on a slip of paper the following information:

Mi pasatiempo favorito es __________.
Lo hago __________ (*frequency/when*).
Me gusta porque __________.

Collect the slips and read them in batches of 4-5 to the class, asking students to guess the identities of the people according to the pastime.

F. Preterite questions. Here are some simple questions you can use to remind students of these forms. These work well as warm-up questions.

1. ¿A qué hora estudiaste anoche?
2. ¿Adónde fuiste después de clase ayer?

3. ¿Comiste en un restaurante ayer?
4. ¿Hablaste por teléfono con alguien? ¿Con quién?
5. ¿Tomaste té o café esta mañana?
6. ¿Cuándo saliste de casa esta mañana?
7. ¿Viste televisión anoche? ¿Qué programa(s) viste?

G. Dictado. Dictations are an excellent listening practice if sentences are read in "chunks" of at least three words at a time. It's a good idea to have one student to the side blackboard while the others do the dictation at their seats. It's crucial that students get immediate feedback, so check them right away. Dictate once in the chunks as indicated, then tell the students the number of words in the sentence, and repeat it one more time.

1. Compré un suéter amarillo / para mi primo Carlos / y creo que le va a gustar. (15)
2. Juanita lavó los platos, / Pepe pasó la aspiradora / y yo saqué toda la basura. (14)
3. Alquilé el apartamento / porque tiene un lavaplatos moderno, / un aire acondicionador muy bueno / y una vista espléndida. (16)
4. Paco se levantó a las seis, / se lavó rápidamente / y se fue a la oficina / sin desayunar. (17)
5. Anteayer Aníbal se acostó / antes de arreglar / el aire acondicionador / de Anita Alonzo, su vecina. (15)

III. GRAMMAR

The following worksheets are in the Student Supplement.

A. El imperfecto: Introducción. (pp. 141-142) This 4-part, art-based worksheet covers four of the most common usages of the imperfect.

B. El imperfecto. (p. 143) 3 cloze passages.

C. Superlatives (I). (p. 144) A 2-part personalized practice with superlative forms. Use as the basis for class discussion.

D. Superlatives (II). (p. 145) An art-based practice.

E. Las palabras interrogativas. (p. 146) Good review of all the question words.

F. Repaso. (pp. 147-149)

IV. INTEGRATIVE ACTIVITIES

These activities are in the Student Supplement.

A. Situaciones. (p. 150) Encourage students to use their scripts as outlines and to speak spontaneously. Call on as many pairs to perform their dialogues as interest/time permits, and ask the class short comprehension questions after each presentation. Review common errors/problems with the whole class after all the performances.

B. Guided Writing: En un parque de Buenos Aires. (p. 151) A picture and accompanying questions. Make sure students get feedback on this exercise. As a follow-up, have them prepare short, spontaneous dialogues between any two characters in the drawing.

C. La familia Ybarra. This art-based information-gap activity practices imperfect and chapter vocabulary. See pp. 153-154 of the Student Supplement for the charts students will work in pairs to complete. Divide students into pairs, and remind them not to look at their partners' sheets as they ask each other questions and fill in the missing information.

V. GAMES

A. Bingó. See p. 152 of the Student Supplement for a preterite Bingo card. This will help keep preterite forms fresh in the students' minds.

CAPÍTULO 10

Communicative Goals for Chapter 10
By the end of the chapter students should be able to:

* talk about their health	☐
* talk about past actions and events	☐
* express reciprocal actions	☐

Grammatical Structures
Students should know:

* reciprocal pronouns	☐
* relative pronouns	☐
* use of the preterite and imperfect	☐

I. PRONUNCIATION

See p. 155 of the Student Supplement for a list of health-related Spanish sayings. Use these for pronunciation practice.

II. LISTENING COMPREHENSION

A. Definiciones. Have students listen to the following sentences and write the appropriate word needed to complete the sentence.

1. Cuando uno come algo, la comida pasa por la __________ antes de llegar al estómago.
2. La tos es síntoma de un __________.
3. Se habla y se come con la __________.
4. El tipo de medicina que se toma para una infección: __________.
5. Se usa la nariz para __________.
6. Se asocia la circulación con el __________.
7. Normalmente se va a un gimnasio para __________.
8. Si el médico quiere que un paciente tome alguna medicina, le da una __________.
9. Si Ud. tiene una temperatura alta, Ud. tiene __________.
10. Lo que uno debe hacer si está muy enfermo y no puede salir de casa: __________.

B. Preguntas personales.

1. ¿Te gustaba ir al médico cuando eras niño/a?
2. ¿Cuántas veces te resfriaste el año pasado?
3. Cuando eras niño/a, ¿qué hacías cuando te enfermabas?
4. ¿Cuándo fue la última vez que fuiste al dentista?
5. ¿Fuiste al médico la última vez que te enfermaste?
6. ¿Tomaste vitaminas esta mañana?
7. ¿Tomabas vitaminas cuando eras niño/a?
8. ¿Qué haces para mantenerte en buen estado de salud?
9. ¿Practicabas mucho deportes cuando estabas en la escuela secundaria?
10. ¿Caminaste a la universidad hoy?
11. ¿Dormiste lo suficiente anoche? ¿Cuántas horas dormiste?

C. Listening Passage: El examen de Juan. Have students read over the **cierto/falso** questions on p. 155 of the Student Supplement. Then read the following passage twice.

Juan no se sentía bien. Tenía un poco de fiebre (*act out*) y le dolían la cabeza y el estómago (*act out*). Lo peor de todo era que tenía un examen de español esa noche y NO quería tomarlo. Juan no era buen estudiante porque no estudiaba casi nunca.

Entonces pensó: "Si voy al hospital porque estoy enfermo, no tengo que tomar el examen," y así Juan fue al hospital. Cuando Juan llegó al hospital, el doctor lo examinó y vio que Juan realmente no estaba muy enfermo. El doctor salió del cuarto y fue a hablar con la doctora de otro paciente. Como Juan quería saber lo que iba a decir el doctor, y no sabía que hablaban de otra persona, se vistió rápidamente y se acercó a los doctores (*act out*) y oyó que hablaban de una operación.

Juan tuvo miedo, y salió corriendo del hospital. "No quiero que me operen," pensó. "Prefiero tomar el examen".

1. A Juan le dolía la cabeza porque estudiaba mucho.
2. Juan decidió ir al hospital porque no quería tomar el examen de español.
3. El médico notó inmediatamente que Juan estaba muy enfermo.
4. Después de ver a Juan, el médico salió del cuarto y habló con otra doctora.
5. Cuando Juan oyó que los dos médicos hablaban de una operación, llamó a su maestro.
6. Juan decidió tomar el examen.

D. <u>Dictado</u>. Read the sentences, pausing according to the slashes. Read each sentence once, tell students the number of words, then repeat the sentence. Review with students.

1. Me dolía todo el cuerpo / y no pude dormir / nada anoche. (11)
2. No me molesta ir al médico, / pero sí me pongo / muy nervioso en el consultorio / del dentista. (17)
3. Si Ud. quiere vivir muchos años, / acuéstese y levántese temprano, / no fume ni tome mucho / y coma con moderación. (18)
4. Para curar el resfriado / es bueno tomar / una limonada caliente / con bastante limón, / un poquito de tequila / y unas dos aspirinas / antes de acostarse. (25)

III. GRAMMAR

The following worksheets are in the Student Supplement.

A. <u>Introduction to Preterite vs. Imperfect</u>. (p. 156) This art-based introduction features a series of questions and answers intended to make students aware of the different uses of the two tenses.

B. <u>El examen de Regina</u>. (p. 157) A cloze passage which students complete based on the accompanying drawings.

C. <u>Una visita al médico</u>. (p. 158) Students are guided to create a short narration using preterite and imperfect.

D. <u>More Preterite vs. Imperfect</u>. (pp. 159-160) Six short cloze passages for extra practice, quizzes, and review.

E. <u>¿Que, quien, quienes o lo que?</u> (p. 161) A relative pronouns practice sheet.

F. <u>Reciprocal pronouns</u>. (p. 162) This cloze passage practices reciprocal actions and preterite vs. imperfect.

G. Repaso. (pp. 163-165)

IV. INTEGRATIVE ACTIVITIES

A. Descriptions in the past. Have students work in pairs. They must pick 4 of the following people and describe the way they were and what they used to do.

EXAMPLE: *Popeye* tenía músculos fuertes, comía mucha espinaca, salía con Olivia y fumaba una pipa.

1. Marilyn Monroe
2. Christopher Columbus
3. Elvis Presley
4. Frida Kahlo
5. Albert Einstein
6. Patsy Cline
7. George Burns
8. Muhammad Ali
9. Selena
10. George Washington

Now have students pick 3 of the following television or movie characters and say something they remember each did one time.

EXAMPLE: Thelma y Louise hicieron un viaje solas.

1. Kramer
2. Cruella de Vil
3. The Nanny
4. The Terminator
5. Luke Skywalker
6. Rambo
7. Homer Simpson
8. Roseanne
9. Indiana Jones

B. Composition. Have students retell any children's fairy tale (*Little Red Riding Hood, Jack in the Beanstalk, Hansel & Gretel*) but with their own original ending. As an example, have them look over *Caperucita Roja* on pp. 320-321 of *Puntos*, paying attention to preterite and imperfect usage in the story. Students should keep their versions to about 100 words. You might use this writing assignment as extra credit. Some of these turn out to be very clever and can be read to the class.

C. Guided Writing: Ayer en el hospital. On p. 166 of the Student Supplement you will find a drawing and accompanying questions. For suggestions on using the Guided Writings, see the Chapter 3 Teacher's Guide.

D. Communicative Goals Practice #3. See p. 168 of the Student Supplement for a picture and a list of topics students can use to practice speaking. Remember, these practices are excellent preparation for oral interviews. See the Chapter 2 Teacher's Guide, p. 16 "Integrative Activities," for more suggestions on using these practices.

E. Encuesta. Have students interview each other asking the three questions below. Then follow-up by asking a few students to report their findings.

1. ¿Dónde estabas cuando ganó las elecciones Bill Clinton?
2. ¿Dónde estabas cuando estalló la bomba en Oklahoma City?
3. ¿Qué hacías cuando supiste el veredicto en el juicio de O. J. Simpson?

V. GAMES

A. Alibi. Tell students that there was a robbery committed last night at Taco Cabana. The police are questioning the suspects and witnesses. For homework, give parts to groups of five students: Two are detectives, three are suspects or witnesses. They must prepare questions if they are playing the role of detective and alibis if they are suspects. Each group performs and then the class votes on who they think did it. In other words, who has the weakest alibi? Listen carefully for the correct use of the preterite and imperfect. Take notes and discuss after each presentation.

B. Bingo. See p. 167 of the Student Supplement for a bingo related to the Chapter 10 themes.

CAPÍTULO 11

Communicative Goals for Chapter 11
By the end of the chapter students should be able to:

* talk about how things are done ☐
* talk about accidents, injuries, and problems ☐
* tell how long something has been happening or how long ago something happened ☐

Grammatical Structures
Students should know:

* adverbs ☐
* **hace...que** ☐
* **se** + indirect object pronoun ☐
* **por y para** ☐

I. PRONUNCIATION

Review the following consonant sounds with students. Then have them practice the sounds and the 6 sentences below in pairs, using the list on p. 169 of the Student Supplement. Each partner should listen carefully for correct pronunciation.

llamo	lleno	lligues	lloro	lluvia
yace	yeso	yi	yoyo	yunque
padre	peso	piña	poco	puso
cada	queque	quiosco	coco	cuna
hado	hecho	hipo	hombre	humo
zaga	cebra	cima	zopo	zurdo
dado	dedo	dido	dodo	dudo

Now have students practice these sentences on p. 169 of the Student Supplement with a partner.

1. Yolanda Illade llevó una blusa amarilla al castillo.
2. Paula puso pocas papas en la parrilla porque su papá las puso en la tortilla ayer.
3. La duquesa quiere quinientos quesos del quiosco de Paquito.
4. Ibiza es una isla sin ni una zona sucia.
5. Ahora hay hasta veinte huéspedes en este hotel hondureño que quieren hielo en sus habitaciones dentro de una hora.
6. David duda que la empleada embarazada haya descansado después de haber subido la escalera.

II. LISTENING COMPREHENSION

A. Dictado. Don't forget to dictate in "chunks" of about 3-5 words. Read the sentence once, tell the students how many words that sentence has, and then repeat it one more time. Have one student go to the side board while the others do the dictation at their seats. Correct after each sentence.

1. En las fiestas / me olvido de los nombres / de las personas / que acabo de conocer. (15)
2. Pablo no se levantó / a las siete / como siempre / sino muy tarde / a las ocho. (15)

3. Oye / ¿trajiste los anuncios del periódico / que te pedí? (9)
4. En esta casita / viven unos amigos míos / que te van a gustar. (11)
5. Lo siento sinceramente / porque sé que no te gusta / que me vuelva a casar. (14)

B. Preguntas personales

1. ¿Puedes aprender el vocabulario de cada capítulo fácilmente?
2. ¿Qué sabes hacer rápidamente? ¿Y qué haces lentamente?
3. ¿Conoces a alguien que hable constantemente? ¿Quién es?
4. Típicamente, ¿para qué hora pones el despertador?
5. ¿Tienes que entregar una composición?
6. ¿Cómo es tu horario este semestre?
7. Cuando estás distraído, ¿se te pierden las cosas más fácilmente?
8. ¿Apagaste todas las luces cuando saliste de casa hoy?
9. ¿Te duele la cabeza hoy?
10. ¿Se te perdió la tarjeta de crédito alguna vez?
11. ¿Se te olvidó la tarea alguna vez este semestre?
12. ¿Cuándo fue la última vez que se te acabó la gasolina?
13. ¿A tu profesor/a de español se le perdieron los exámenes alguna vez?
14. ¿Sufriste muchas presiones en la escuela secundaria?
15. ¿Sufres muchas presiones este semestre? ¿Por qué?

C. Listening passages: Accidentes y travesuras. These short descriptions practice Chapter 11 vocabulary and use of se for unexpected or unplanned events. Have students look at the drawings on p. 170 of the Student Supplement as you read the passages.

INSTRUCTIONS (read to students):

You will hear a series of short passages about the people in the drawings. The first time you listen, identify each person or group by writing their names next to the corresponding drawing. Then second time, listen for the details you need to correct the false statements below.

- ¡Pobre Sr. Villarreal! No miraba por dónde iba y ¡plas! se dio con una puerta. Se cayó al suelo y estuvo inconsciente por cinco minutos.
- Hace dos días que Pedro tiene un dolor de muelas horrible. Le duele tanto que no puede concentrarse. Necesita ir al dentista, pero hoy es imposible, porque tiene que terminar un proyecto importante y la fecha límite es mañana.
- Cristina está muy feliz hoy. ¡Qué amorosos son sus hijos! A ninguno se le olvidó que era el Día de las Madres.
- ¡Qué distraído está Jorge últimamente! Hoy, por ejemplo, se le olvidó quitar la cafetera de la estufa. Debería tener más cuidado.
- ¡Qué mala suerte! Fernanda y Juan fueron a la playa pero empezó a llover. Para colmo, se les quedaron sus jerseys en casa, y pasaron mucho frío.
- Isa es una chica muy responsable y le encanta su trabajo. Sin embargo, últimamente anda muy deprimida. Parece que tiene una jefa nueva que le da demasiado trabajo, y por eso está sufriendo muchas presiones ahorita.

- Acaban de llegar muchos amigos a la casa de Roberto, y él no sabe qué decirles ahora. Ellos quisieron hacerle una fiesta de sorpresa para su cumpleaños, pero -- ¡qué sorpresa para ellos! -- se equivocaron de la fecha. El cumpleaños de Roberto es el 15 de mayo, no el 14.

D. Definiciones

1. Lo que subes para ir de un piso de un edificio a otro:
2. Lo opuesto de poner un aparato o la luz:
3. El día en que se debe entregar algo, como un trabajo:
4. Necesitas esto para conducir o abrir una puerta:
5. La cosa que te despierta por la mañana:
6. Lo que debes hacer cuando has cometido un error:
7. Si se te caen o se te rompen las cosas con frecuencia, a lo mejor eres una persona ___.
8. Cuando sientes mucho de esto, es casi imposible relajarte.

III. GRAMMAR

The following worksheets are in the Student Supplement.

A. ¿Cuanto tiempo hace que...? (p. 171) A two-part personalized worksheet, practicing with ongoing and past actions.

B. Unplanned/Unexpected events with "se". (p. 172) Students often have difficulty with this structure, and this translation chart is helpful.

C. "Se" for unplanned events. (p. 173) Use after presenting the "se" structure. A two-part worksheet.

D. ¿Qué tienen? ¿Qué les pasó? (p. 174) This two-page art-based practice incorporates the "se" structure for unplanned events and Chapter 11 vocabulary. Assign as homework and have students write their sentences on the board the next day as review.

E. Por vs. para. (p. 175) This sheet of English sentences helps students distinguish between the different meanings of **por** and **para**.

F. ¿Por o para? (p. 176) A fill-in-the-blank activity.

G. Repaso: Capítulo 11. (pp. 177-180)

IV. INTEGRATIVE ACTIVITIES

A. Situaciones. Have students get together with a classmate and prepare a dialogue based on one of the following topics.

- One person arrives an hour late for the first date with the girl/guy of his/her dreams.
- One person is absent from Spanish class the day of the final exam.
- One person returns to work after lunch at 3:30 p.m. on his/her first day of work.

Give students some guidance. In each case, one student will be the person doing the questioning (i.e., date, Spanish teacher, boss) and one will be the person doing the explaining. Have students set up a conversation in which they talk about what happened and then resolve the situation. Ask students to use the vocabulary from this chapter on pp. 329-330 of *Puntos* and the expressions on p. 337. They should be creative with the content of the dialogue.

B. Guided Writing: ¿Qué pasó hoy en el centro? See p. 181 of the Student Supplement for the picture and accompanying questions.

V. GAMES

A. 20 Preguntas. This version of the game will based on the ghosts of famous people so students can use the past tense. You should do a sample first. Have students work in pairs to prepare 5 possible questions for this game.

EXAMPLE: ¿Fuiste cantante, actor, político o artista, etcétera.?
¿Viajaste a muchos países durante tu carrera?
¿Eras muy famoso cuando te moriste?

B. Verb Wheel. You'll need 8 or 9 dice for this game. Give one die to each group of 3 students. The first student rolls the die to determine the person (Wheel 1), the second student rolls for the verb (Wheel 2) and the third rolls for the tense or mood (Wheel 3). Students must write the numbers they rolled and then produce the correct forms.

EXAMPLE:	3 / 2 / 4	No quiero que ella se caiga.
	4 / 5 / 5	Nosotros vamos a acostarnos.

Students must come up with 10 sentences. The first group to finish wins. While the others are finishing have the winners put the numbers on the board and their corresponding sentences.

VERB WHEELS

Wheel 1

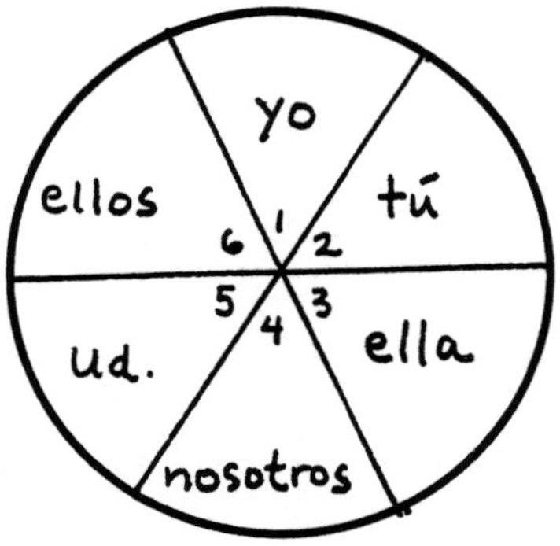

Wheel 2

Wheel 3

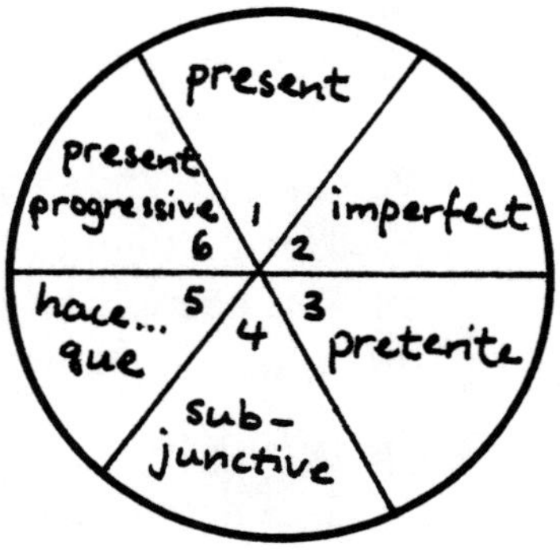

CAPÍTULO 12

Communicative Goals for Chapter 12
By the end of the chapter students should be able to:

* talk about modern technology	☐
* describe where they live	☐
* tell others what to do	☐
* express desires and requests	☐

Grammatical Structures
Students should know:

* informal commands	☐
* use of the subjunctive for influence	☐

I. PRONUNCIATION

A. Practice pronunciation and Chapter 12 vocabulary simultaneously using this word-association game. Start the game by saying a part of a house **(la alcoba)**, and then point to a student. The student repeats the word, adds on another word associated in meaning **(la alcoba, la cama)**, and points to another student, who repeats and adds on another word. Continue until the chain of associated words becomes too long to remember or until a student cannot add on a logical word. Practice each day with a different part of the house.

B. See p. 183 of the Student Supplement for pronunciation practice sentences.

II. LISTENING COMPREHENSION

A. Cierto/Falso. Use these statements and the definitions below as warm-up, daily listening comprehension practice or vocabulary review.

1. Un contestador automático cuesta menos que una computadora.
2. El dinero que ganamos es el alquiler.
3. Necesitas una impresora para hacer copias de un trabajo escrito en una computadora.
4. Si recibes un aumento de sueldo, recibes menos dinero.
5. Puedes ver películas en tu casa usando tu equipo fotográfico.
6. Los peces viven en un acuario.
7. Un cartel es como una foto o una pintura muy grande.
8. Una moto es más grande que un monopatín.
9. Los atletas profesionales no tienen muchos trofeos.
10. Si tu computadora falla, debes apagarla y ponerla de nuevo.

B. Definiciones

1. El dinero que una persona recibe por el trabajo que hace.
2. Un animal que vive en el agua.
3. Una forma de transporte que no usa gasolina; a veces tiene diez velocidades.
4. Lo que pones si quieres escuchar un poco de música.
5. Lo que tienes si te gusta sacar fotos.
6. Un tipo de coche grande, muy útil para llevar cosas o para una familia con muchos hijos.
7. Lo que debes pedirle a tu jefe si quieres más dinero.
8. La forma en que se paga el sueldo.

9. Un aparato que usamos para ver una película en casa o para ver un programa de televisión más tarde.
10. Se usa si no se tiene la energía para levantarse y cambiar de canal.
11. El aparato que permite que recibas mensajes telefónicos cuando no estás en casa.
12. Un tipo de carta que llega por computadora.
13. Un tipo de computadora que puedes llevar contigo a clase.
14. La persona a quien le pagas el alquiler de tu apartamento.
15. Lo opuesto de las afueras.
16. Un tipo de edificio universitario donde viven los estudiantes.
17. La persona que vive cerca de ti.
18. Un sinónimo para barrio.
19. La persona que trabaja en una casa de apartamentos y que ayuda a los inquilinos.

C. Un apartamento nuevo. The script below describes a new apartment. Read to the students as they complete the answer sheet on the bottom of p. 183 in the Student Supplement.

INSTRUCTIONS (read to students):

You and your friend Diego are looking for a new place to live and Diego has just gone to look at an apartment. Listen to what he says about the place. On the left, list the apartment's good points; on the right, list the bad points.

¿Sabes? No me gustó mucho ese apartamento. Está en las afueras y bastante lejos de la ruta de cualquier autobús. Pero el alquiler es muy razonable -- sólo $250.00 al mes, luz y gas incluidos. El apartamento está en el tercer piso y hay una terraza bonita con vista. Las vecinas son unas chicas muy simpáticas. ¿Qué más? Ah -- no se permiten animales, así no sé qué podríamos hacer con los gatos. Hay una piscina, pero es pequeña y estaba bastante sucia.

D. Preguntas. Use to warm-up, review vocabulary and structures, or to begin a class discussion.

1. ¿Cuáles son las ventajas de tener una videocasetera?
2. ¿Qué cosas necesitas para decorar tu casa?
3. ¿Tienes muchos carteles? ¿De qué estilo?
4. ¿Tu apartamento es perfecto? ¿Qué defectos tiene?
5. ¿Tienes un trabajo? ¿Cómo es?
6. ¿Cómo es tu jefe?
7. ¿Cuál es mejor, trabajar o ser estudiante?
8. ¿Cómo son las residencias universitarias?
9. ¿Qué recomiendas que yo haga este fin de semana?
10. ¿Tienes una computadora? ¿Cuándo la usas?
11. ¿Por qué es bueno tener un walkman?
12. ¿Qué quieres que tus padres te compren para tu alcoba?
13. ¿Dónde recomiendas que un estudiante nuevo viva en (*your town/city*)?
14. ¿Te gusta navegar la red?
15. ¿Tienes una bicicleta? ¿La usas para venir a la universidad?
16. ¿Qué haces cuando tu computadora falla?
17. ¿Piensas que los teléfonos del coche son necesarios?

E. Discrimination Drill: Present, past or subjunctive? Now that subjunctive has been presented, students can get their verb forms confused. This discrimination drill is good practice. For more practice you may also want to do a discrimination drill similar to the one in the Chapter 7 Teacher's Guide, p. 45. First have students prepare a sheet with these three symbols written on top:

X = present/actual ← = past **?** = subjunctive

Then read the following pairs of sentences and have students write the symbol indicating the tense or mood of the sentence they hear. Review afterward.

1. Quiero que mi hermana llegue temprano.
2. Mi hermana llegó muy tarde.

1. Marta trabaja en un supermercado.
2. Trabajamos hasta la medianoche ayer.

1. El dueño prefiere que no tengamos animales.
2. Me gusta vivir cerca de la universidad.

1. Salió a las ocho menos cuarto.
2. Mi primo sale con Rosa Pérez.

1. La universidad insiste en que paguemos la matrícula hoy.
2. Pagamos las cuentas hace tres días.

1. Saqué la basura tres veces la semana pasada.
2. Saca la basura todos los lunes.

F. ¿Sí o no? This listening comprehension activity helps students distinguish between affirmative and negative informal commands. The script follows, and students will use the answer sheet on the top part of p. 184 in the Student Supplement.

INSTRUCTIONS (read to students):

In the co-op where Miguel lives, everyone usually shares duties. But during finals week, people are too busy to help out, so they all ask poor Miguel to fill in. Listen as I read the messages Miguel's housemates have left on his door. You will hear the messages twice. The first time, indicate whether his housemates are telling him to do or not to do the things in the list. The second time you hear the messages, listen for the answers to the true-false statements.

- Miguel, cariño, hazme un favor. Lávame los platos esta noche y te los lavo mañana. Gracias, Carmen.
- Miguel, por favor, no vayas a la biblioteca antes de las siete. Necesito que cocines esta noche porque no puedo hacerlo. No prepares la carne, porque la vamos a comer mañana. Gracias, Roque.
- ¡Miguel, ayúdame! Estoy desesperada. Saca la basura y pasa la aspiradora. Tengo que estudiar. Mil gracias, Rosa.

- Miguel, un favorcito... Por favor, ve al supermercado y haz la compra para esta semana. La lista está en mi cuarto. No olvides la leche. Gracias, hombre. Víctor.
- Miguel, hay un problema con el agua del baño. Por favor, llama al plomero y dile que venga en seguida. No le pagues hoy - le pagaremos después. Gracias, Sancho.
- Miguel, estoy en crisis. Por favor, límpiame el baño. No pude hacerlo esta tarde. Muchas gracias, Marta.

G. Dictado. Teaching negative commands is a good opportunity for practicing spelling of subjunctive forms. Dictate the following commands to the class, asking one student to write the sentences at the board. Do not read too slowly and pause where the slashes appear. After reading each command once, tell students how many words are in the sentence, then repeat once more. Review errors immediately with students.

1. Susana, juega en el patio; / / no juegues en casa. (9)
2. Diego, llega temprano mañana; / / no llegues después de las nueve. (10)
3. Raúl, háblame en español; / / no me hables en inglés. (9)
4. Laura, hazme un favor; / / no hagas tu tarea durante la clase. (11)
5. Pablo, ve al parque; / / no vayas al cine. (8)
6. Teresa, dime la respuesta; / / no se la digas a Julia. (10)
7. Marcos, pon tu composición aquí; / / no la pongas allí. (9)
8. Lola, saca tu libro; / / no saques tu manual de ejercicios. (10)
9. Juan, escúchame ahora; / / no escuches la radio. (7)

III. GRAMMAR

Note: Students can get frustrated with the concept of the subjunctive. Remind them that they will see more of the subjunctive in later chapters. You may find the worksheets included in the Student Supplement and the following tips for teaching the subjunctive helpful.

SOME TIPS FOR TEACHING THE SUBJUNCTIVE

Below are three suggestions for introducing the subjunctive.

1. Have students work in pairs for this problem-solving activity. Ask them to figure out how the sentences in column A differ from those in column B.

A	B
1. Pepe fuma.	1. Su mamá no quiere que él fume.
2. José sale con Mari.	2. Recomiendo que José no salga con Mari.
3. Inés nunca come carne.	3. Su mamá quiere que Inés coma carne.
4. Volvemos tarde.	4. Mamá prefiere que volvamos temprano.

Students should notice that the sentences in column B have **2 subjects**, **que**, and that the **verb ending** in the second part of the sentence is new. You can then explain the concept of verbs of influence and the mechanics of forming the subjunctive endings. Since this is the first time students have seen the subjunctive, stick to verbs of influence (**querer**, **insistir en**, **preferir**, **recomendar**) until they get the concept down.

2. Now draw 2 figures (stick figures of a mother and son) on the board and explain to the students that the mother wants her son to do the chores she usually does herself because she is feeling very sick today.

Mamá

Pepe

Normalmente mamá hace muchas cosas, pero hoy está muy enferma y su hijo, Pepe, tiene que ayudarla.

Normalmente **mamá** limpia la casa, pero hoy **mamá** quiere que **Pepe** limpie la casa.
Normalmente **mamá** trabaja en el jardín, pero hoy...
Normalmente **mamá** prepara la cena, pero hoy...
Normalmente **mamá** sirve la comida, pero hoy...
Normalmente **mamá** lava los platos, pero hoy...

Do the first one and then give students a minute to do the next four. Then ask the question: Is her son actually doing these chores, or does the mom want her son to do them? Since it's the latter, we can't use the indicative, which is used to state facts. We must use the subjunctive.

3. The Gun Analogy. This is a strange way to explain the mechanics of the subjunctive, but it can be a funny and helpful visual reminder.

Tell students that there are many trigger verbs and trigger expressions that they should begin to recognize. We will just concentrate on the trigger verbs of influence at first: **querer**, **insistir en**, **preferir**, **recomendar**, **desear**. Under certain circumstances these trigger verbs can cause quite a disturbance. When the trigger verb causes the trigger to be pulled, the red flag falls out with "QUE" on it and the explosion blows off the end of the second verb. It must be replaced with a different ending.

The following worksheets are in the Student Supplement.

A. Reference Sheet for Commands. (p. 185) Students find this sheet, which presents **tú** and **Ud./Uds.** command forms for common verbs, quite helpful.

B. Informal commands. (p. 186) These questions elicit informal commands and object pronouns in the responses and incorporate Chapter 12 vocabulary.

C. Mandatos y consejos. (p. 187) A personalized pair activity practicing with informal commands. Review answers as a class.

D. WEIRDO: When to Use the Subjunctive. (p. 188) This handy reference sheet summarizes the use of the subjunctive in noun clauses in cases of will/wish, emotion, impersonal expressions, requests, doubt/denial, and ojalá.

E. El subjuntivo. (p. 189) A two-part worksheet.

F. Subjunctive with **tú** vs. **tú** commands. (p. 190) This worksheet contrasts these usages.

G. Subjunctive: ¿Qué me recomiendas? (p. 191) Students help solve their Spanish teachers' problems using **recomendar** and the subjunctive. Assign as homework and see how many different recommendations students make for each problem.

H. Práctica: Present, Preterite, Subjunctive. (p. 192) This drill worksheet contrasts the forms for common verbs.

I. Repaso. (pp. 193-195)

IV. INTEGRATIVE ACTIVITIES

A. "Dos Minutos." In preparation for final oral interviews, have students chat with a partner for two minutes each day from now on. On a Monday you can tell them to do small talk, then on other days you can suggest a topic: **1) las clases, 2) el compañero de cuarto, 3) el fin de semana, 4) la residencia, 5) un viaje.** Have a student with a timer watch keep track of the two minutes. S/he should say "Preparados, listos, ya" and then call time with "Ya." Then call on one or two pairs to perform.

B. "¿Cómo es tu apartamento/casa/cuarto?" This is a fun exercise in which students form pairs and describe their houses/rooms to each other and draw each other's living spaces. Start out by briefly describing your own place with one of your better students at the board drawing. Put useful phrases on the board and remind students to use prepositions like **a la derecha de/encima de**.

C. "¿Qué tienes y qué quieres?" A fun group discussion/poll activity. Begin by writing this question on the board. then answer for yourself: "Tengo muchos libros. Quiero un perro." Then ask students the same question. Write down responses on the board in some type of poll format. To keep the activity from becoming monotonous, use follow-up questions; also ask students to tell you about what other students want/have. (e.g.: "Bubba, ¿qué cosa tiene Susie? ¿Y qué cosa quiere comprar? Y ¿por qué no lo puede comprar ahora?") and so forth. At the end, try to draw some kind of consensus regarding your class.

OJO This activity can be turned into an excellent subjunctive practice. Use the statements made by students and have the class react or respond to them by using the subjunctive. Here is an example: Bubba says: "Quiero una casa muy grande." Someone says: "Es importante que Bubba compre una casa." or "Es horrible que no tenga una casa."

D. Guided Writing: En una zona residencial de San Antonio. See p. 197 of the Student Supplement for the picture and questions.

V. GAMES

A. Bingo. (Student Supplement, p. 196)

CAPÍTULO 13

Communicative Goals for Chapter 13
By the end of the chapter students should be able to:

* talk about the arts and culture	☐
* express emotions	☐
* express disbelief and doubt	☐
* rank things	☐

Grammatical Structures
Students should know:

* use of subjunctive for emotions	☐
* use of subjunctive for uncertainty	☐
* ordinal numbers	☐

I. PRONUNCIATION

See p. 201 of the Student Supplement for a pronunciation practice working with the new chapter vocabulary and vowel sounds.

II. LISTENING COMPREHENSION

A. <u>Descriptions: ¿Qué deben hacer estas personas?</u> Read the descriptions below of the cultural interests of different people as students complete the chart on p. 199 of the Student Supplement. As a follow-up, have students explain why they recommended a particular activity for each person.

INSTRUCTIONS (read to students):

Listen as I describe the interests of 5 different people. Based on what you hear, indicate which cultural activity would be the best for each person in the chart in your Supplement. Explain why you recommend that activity, as well.

- A Diego le gustaría ser dramaturgo famoso algún día. En la universidad, estudió todas las obras de Shakespeare, Calderón, Tennessee Williams y Federico García Lorca.
- Leonor tiene una gran colección de bolsas y blusas hechas a mano de México. Le gusta observar a los artesanos y aprender cómo hacen sus artesanías tradicionales.
- José estudia arquitectura en la universidad, y por lo tanto le interesan bastante las obras de los arquitectos europeos.
- A Sarita le fascinan las ruinas de las antiguas civilizaciones. A ella le gustaría estudiar la historia y la antropología precolombianas en la universidad.
- Maribel es cantante, y le encanta todo lo relacionado a la música. El año pasado, tuvo la oportunidad de conocer a Pavarroti, el gran tenor italiano. Algún día espera conocer a Plácido Domingo y José Carreras también.

B. <u>Descriptions: ¿Adónde fueron y qué hicieron?</u> This listening comprehension activity practices new Chapter 13 vocabulary while recycling preterite forms. Have students listen to the descriptions of different people's trips as they complete the chart on p. 200 of the Student Supplement.

INSTRUCTIONS (read to students):

I will read some short descriptions of what 6 different people did on vacation. As you listen, complete the chart in your Supplement by writing the name of each person next to the place s/he visited on vacation. Then write one thing the person did in that place.

- El año pasado, Héctor fue a México para hacer investigaciones para un libro sobre las civilizaciones precolombianas. Mientras estuvo en la capital, Héctor visitó el Museo de Antropología allí. En el museo, vio muchos objetos y artefactos de los aztecas, mayas y toltecas.
- Cuando era niña, Fernanda siempre quería ser bailarina. Así que cuando ella visitó la capital, consiguió entradas para ver el famosísimo Ballet Folklórico de México. A Fernanda le encantó el espectáculo, y compró un cartel hermoso del Ballet Folklórico como recuerdo de la experiencia.
- A Juan Luis siempre le interesaba el baile también, aunque--¡pobre!--la verdad es que nunca tenía mucho talento para el baile. Sin embargo, el año pasado durante un viaje a España, Juan Luis tomó unas lecciones de baile flamenco.
- Alicia es artista, y le encanta la pintura. De modo que cuando ella y su esposo fueron a España, ella quiso visitar todos los museos. Claro que vieron el Museo del Prado, pero también fueron a Toledo para ver algunas pinturas y la casa de El Greco.
- Como es arquitecto, a Joaquín le fascina la arquitectura romana. Durante su viaje a España, visitó varios lugares donde había ruinas romanas. A Joaquín le pareció increíble el aqueducto romano de Segovia, y sacó muchísimas fotos de este monumento famoso.
- A Teresa le aburren los museos y los monumentos. Cuando está de viaje, prefiere salir a la calle, ver gente e ir de compras. Cuando Teresa estuvo en México, visitó varios mercados. El que más le gustó a ella fue el mercado de artesanías en Oaxaca, donde compró muchos tejidos y blusas bordadas como regalos para sus amigas.

C. Definiciones

1. La materia que uno necesita estudiar para saber construir casas y edificios.
2. La persona que escribe obras teatrales.
3. La persona que escribe poemas.
4. La persona que hace formas o figuras de barro, cerámica, mármol.
5. El lugar donde hay edificios antiguos.
6. Un tipo de poema, pero que se canta.
7. El tipo de obra en la que típicamente cantan Luciano Pavarotti, Cecilia Bártoli y Plácido Domingo.
8. La persona que les dice qué tienen que hacer a los actores.
9. Lo que deben memorizar los actores.
10. Un tipo de baile muy elegante y estilizado.
11. El rock, la salsa, el jazz y el tejano son todos tipos de __________.
12. Una expresión para describir una obra de arte realmente magnífica.

D. Preguntas personales

1. ¿Te gusta bailar? ¿Sabes bailar unos bailes latinos?

2. ¿Vas al cine mucho? ¿Qué tipo de película te interesa?
3. ¿Te gusta el cine extranjero?
4. ¿Qué tipo de música prefieres escuchar?
5. ¿Escuchas música mientras estudias? ¿Tienes un estéreo en casa?
6. ¿Sabes cantar? Cuando estás en tu coche, ¿cantas cuando tocan tus canciones favoritas en la radio?
7. ¿Cantabas en el coro de tu escuela o iglesia cuando eras niño?
8. ¿Qué te gusta escribir? ¿Cuentos, poesía, artículos, ensayos, cartas...?
9. ¿Tomas una clase de literatura este semestre? ¿Qué tienes que leer para esa clase?
10. ¿Estudiaste literatura también en el colegio? ¿Qué obras leíste?
11. ¿Cuántos dramas de Shakespeare conoces?
12. ¿Qué te gusta leer en tus ratos libres?
13. ¿Crees que las novelas de autores populares como Stephen King o Danielle Steele son "literatura"? ¿Por qué sí o no?
14. ¿Leíste alguna vez una novela o un cuento de un escritor latinoamericano? ¿Cuál?
15. ¿Crees que tienes mucho talento artístico?
16. Después de clases hoy, ¿qué necesitas hacer primero? ¿Segundo?
17. ¿Te gusta que Uds. los estudiantes tengan que estudiar otro idioma?
18. ¿Te gusta que tengamos exámenes? ¿Te molesta que yo les dé mucha tarea?

III. GRAMMAR

The following worksheets are in the Student Supplement.

A. Subjunctive Sentence Structure. (p. 202) A simple explanation that contrasts subjunctive and indicative sentences.

B. El subjuntivo y las emociones. (p. 203) This personalized worksheet can be assigned in pairs or for homework; do a class review of the different responses.

C. Subjunctive of Doubt and Denial. (p. 204) This practice contrasts the use of subjunctive and indicative with expressions such as **Creo que/No creo que**.

D. ¿Subjuntivo o indicativo? (pp. 205-206) Two fill-in-the-blank worksheets.

E. El subjuntivo: Frases incompletas. (p. 207) This sentence-completion worksheet practices all the uses of the subjunctive presented so far.

F. Subjunctive Trigger Phrases. (p. 208) This worksheet contrasts clauses which require the subjunctive with those that are followed by the indicative.

G. Prepositions and infinitives. (p. 209) A reference sheet and some practice sentences.

H. Repaso. (pp. 210-212)

Here are two subjunctive vs. indicative passages to use for extra practice or quizzes.

1. Hoy hay una enorme venta de liquidación en el almacén Sears. El director del almacén, Mario Benítez, espera que muchas personas (venir) _______________ a comprar miles de cosas y por eso ha rebajado todos los precios. Para darles una buena impresión a los clientes, Mario insiste en que todos los empleados (vestirse) _______________ bien y no les permite que (fumar) _______________ durante las horas de trabajo. Él dice que los buenos empleados (tener) _______________ la oportunidad de recibir un "bonus" si todo va bien. A muchos de los empleados no les gusta que Mario (ser) _______________ tan estricto pero saben que (ser) _______________ necesario. Es evidente que Mario (tomar) _______________ en serio su trabajo. Pero muchos creen que Mario (ser) _______________ demasiado nervioso para ser un buen director. Él dice que es importante que todos (vender) _______________ mucho porque vendieron muy poco en la venta de liquidación en enero. ¡Ojalá que (salir) _______________ bien esta venta!

2. Mi amiga Juanita siempre dice que su vida (ser) _______________ muy difícil. Y es verdad... La pobre trabaja con un jefe horrible, un hombre que se llama Lorenzo. Lorenzo es un idiota... es increíble que alguien tan estúpido (ganar) _______________ tanto dinero y (tener) _______________ un puesto tan importante. A Juanita no le gusta que Lorenzo (tratar) _______________ tan mal a los empleados. Nunca les dice "Por favor" cuando quiere que (hacer - ellos) _______________ algo. Siempre cambia de idea (*changes his mind*), pero después dice que sus empleados no (entender) _______________ nada. Juanita quiere (encontrar) _______________ otro trabajo... ¡qué lástima que la situación económica (estar) _______________ tan mala en estos días! Espero que ella (poder) _______________ renunciar su puesto pronto, porque sé que Lorenzo no (ir) _______________ a cambiar nunca.

IV. INTEGRATIVE ACTIVITIES

A. Diálogos: Capítulo 13. See p. 213 of the Student Supplement for two chapter-related dialogue topics.

B. Sondeo: Las artes. See p. 214 of the Student Supplement for the chart students should complete as they poll classmates about their cultural interests. Allow 5-6 minutes for students to poll one another, and then review interests and opinions as a class.

C. Guided Writing: Planes para el fin de semana. The picture and questions are on p. 216 of the Student Supplement.

V. GAMES

A. Bingo. See p. 215 of the Student Supplement for a Chapter 13 bingo card.

B. Password. Password works well for this chapter since there is so much concrete vocabulary.

C. ¿Quién soy? Make name tags of famous artists, writers, actors, etc., and put one on the back of each student. Students circulate and ask yes/no questions about themselves to find out their identity. Here are some possible names to use:

Goya
Picasso
da Vinci
Emily Dickinson
Frida Kahlo
Cervantes
Gabriel García Márquez
William Shakespeare
I. M. Pei
Maya Angelou
Tennessee Williams
Meryl Streep
Marlon Brando
Federico García Lorca
Jane Austen
Mikhail Baryshnikov

Frank Lloyd Wright
Andy Warhol
Katharine Hepburn
Ludwig von Beethoven

D. Categorías. Divide the class into 4 teams, and have each team form rows next to the chalkboard, with team members sitting behind another in a line. Call the first student from each team to the board, and give them one of the categories below. Give students 30 seconds to write the name of a person who fits that category. After writing a name, the student returns to his/her team's line and goes to the back of the line. The next students in line for each team go to the board for the next category. The team with the most correct answers wins after all the categories have been called out.

Possible categories:

un dramaturgo famoso
una novela muy larga
un pintor español
un novelista latinoamericano
un cuadro muy famoso
unas ruinas aztecas
un bailarín/una bailarina famoso/a
un director de cine
un actor/una actriz mexicano/a
un pintor americano del siglo XX
un museo europeo
un cantante de ópera

CAPÍTULO 14

Communicative Goals for Chapter 14
By the end of the chapter students should be able to:

* talk about the environment	☐
* talk about cars	☐
* describe conditions	☐
* tell what they have or have not done recently	☐

Grammatical Structures
Students should know:

* past participles used as adjectives	☐
* present perfect indicative	☐
* present perfect subjunctive	☐

I. PRONUNCIATION

A. Practice Chapter 14 cognates by having students listen carefully to the following words and repeat them, trying to avoid English pronunciation and intonation.

el tráfico	la policía
la licencia	el carro
la estación	la ambulancia
la gasolina	la batería
el accidente	el límite
el tanque	el pedal
el aire	aparcar
el motor	la presión
la transmisión	automática
manual	la circulación

B. The poem by Gabriela Mistral on p. 458 of *Puntos* is good for pronunciation practice and memorization. Have students listen and repeat as you recite the poem, then have pairs alternate reading verses to each other. Circulate and work with students on sounds especially difficult for beginners: **r**, initial and intervocalic **d**, etc.

II. LISTENING COMPREHENSION

A. "<u>El medio ambiente.</u>" This passage describes what a group of friends does to protect the environment. Read the passage to the students and have them fill in the chart on p. 217 of the Student Supplement. NOTE: This works well as a preliminary to the environmental discussion in INTEGRATIVE ACTIVITIES. The first time students hear the passage, they should check off the actions mentioned. The second time, they should listen for the person doing the action. Remind students that they will not need to understand every word in order to complete the chart, and that many of the terms they will hear are cognates. You can ask them to listen for the Spanish words for the following: *crisis*, *recycling center*, *insecticide*, *organic*, *methods*, *electricity*, *chemical products*, *biodegradable*.

¡Hola! Me llamo Juanita. Mis amigos y yo estamos muy preocupados por la crisis del medio ambiente, y todos hacemos un esfuerzo por no causar más problemas.

Por ejemplo, una cosa que hago es reciclar. Reciclo vidrio y latas. A veces es una molestia, porque soy muy perezosa y espero hasta que haya un montón de latas en mi terraza, y después llevo todo a un centro de reciclaje.

Mi novio Guillermo tiene un jardín detrás de su casa. Él está en contra de las insectidicas, y por eso su jardín es totalmente orgánico. Mata los insectos por métodos naturales en vez de usar productos químicos peligrosos. Parece increíble, pero las verduras de su jardín están más sanas y grandes que las de cualquier supermercado. Otra cosa que hace él es ir a la universidad en bicicleta, en vez de tomar el autobús.

Otro amigo mío, Diego, conserva electricidad como sea. Toma duchas rapidísimas y casi nunca pone el aire acondicionador, aun cuando hace bastante calor. También compró unas bombillas especiales para las lámparas que duran más tiempo y que gastan menos electricidad.

Mi amiga Gianna no compra productos químicos domésticos como Clorox o Lysol. Usa productos biodegradables cuando sea posible, y para cuidar a sus animales (tiene dos perros y tres gatos) usa un champú orgánico para matar las pulgas.

B. "En la playa." Read the description below as students listen while looking over the accompanying picture on p. 218 of the Student Supplement. The first time students hear the passage, they identify the people in the picture. During the second reading, students listen for answers to the questions at the bottom of the picture.

Hay mucha gente hoy en la playa de Puntarenas. Por ejemplo, han venido dos turistas alemanes, Max y Mónika. Los pobres han tomado demasiado sol y ahora están totalmente quemados. Mañana van a tener que quedarse en el hotel, ¿verdad? Pero por suerte, Carlos y su novia Laura no están quemados, porque Laura se ha acordado de traer su sombrilla. Ella trabaja en un biblioteca, y siempre tiene todo muy bien organizado. En este momento, Carlos y Laura están sentados, mirando a su alrededor. Carlos está enojado porque algunos niños han tirado arena encima de su toalla.

También han venido los Gómez a la playa. Van a pasar todo el día aquí, y la hija, Teresa Gómez, está muy ilusionada. ¡Le encante la playa! Su padre, el Sr. Gómez, ha alquilado una sombrilla y su mamá, la Sra. Gómez, ha preparado un almuerzo delicioso.

El Sr. Verde ha venido hoy también, como siempre, y ha traído sus binóculos. Le gusta mirar a todos muy cerca, aunque a los demás no les gusta que él los mire así. Ya esta mañana tres señoras le han pedido que se fuera a otro lugar.

También están hoy los hermanos, Daniel y Sara. Viven cerca de la playa y por eso vienen aquí casi todos los días. A Daniel le gusta jugar en la arena, y esta mañana ha construido tres castillos. Ahora está terminando el cuarto. A su hermana Sara le fascinan los animalitos que se encuentran a veces en la playa. Ya ha encontrado unas estrellas de mar y ahora acaba de encontrar un lindo cangrejo para llevar a su mamá.

Como siempre, está aquí Ramón, el salvavidas. Ramón ha trabajado aquí muchos años. Es un muchacho muy cuidadoso y nunca ha habido ningún accidente durante sus horas de trabajo.

Por fin, tenemos a Alejo y a Juanita. Se han conocido hoy mismo, en la playa. Ahora están jugando al disco volador y han decidido ir después a comer a un restaurante de mariscos que está cerca. ¡Qué romántico!

C. Dictado. The present perfect, introduced in Chapter 14, can be difficult to understand for beginning students because the vowel sounds often seem to "blend" together. Dictate the following sentences to the class while one student writes the sentences at the board. Read the sentences according to the pauses shown, but don't speak too slowly. After reading each sentence once, tell the students the number of words in it, and read the sentence again. Correct the errors right away.

1. Yo sé qué has hablado / con la consejera, / pero ¿has pagado la matrícula también? (14)
2. Rafael me ha ayudado / a escribir esta composición. (8)
3. ¿Qué has hecho / esta mañana, Alicia? (6)
4. Pues, he hecho las camas / y he ido al mercado Oriental. (11)
5. ¿Quién aquí ha usado / una computadora? (6)
6. Ojalá que ella / no se haya aburrido / en la fiesta. (10)
7. Espero que Elena / haya encontrado / el otro hotel. (8)
8. Ya he empezado / el trabajo / para el lunes. (8)

D. Preguntas personales. Use these questions for warm-up, discussions, or for the listening part of pop quizzes.

1. ¿Qué es algo que te encanta hacer?
2. ¿A veces madrugas para terminar tu tarea o estudiar para un examen?
3. ¿Qué medio de transporte usas frecuentemente?
4. ¿Hay algún lugar contaminado en (*your city/area/region*)?
5. ¿Te gusta estar con mucha gente o prefieres la soledad?
6. ¿Has vivido en o visitado una ciudad grande?
7. ¿Prefieres la ciudad o el campo?
8. ¿Cuáles son las ventajas/desventajas de vivir en (*your city/area/region*)?
9. ¿Qué has hecho esta mañana?
10. ¿Qué película buena/mala has visto recientemente?
11. ¿Has ido a comer a un restaurante chino/mexicano/italiano esta semana?
12. ¿Qué planes has hecho para el fin de semana?
13. ¿Has conocido a alguien famoso?
14. ¿Qué haces para proteger el medio ambiente?
15. ¿Tienes un coche? ¿Cómo es?
16. ¿Qué es lo bueno de tener un coche? ¿Y lo malo?
17. ¿Conoces a un buen mecánico? ¿Cómo se llama?
18. ¿Crees que en este país dependemos demasiado de los coches?
19. En tu opinión, ¿es posible que lleguemos a tener coches eléctricos para el año 2000?
20. ¿Prefieres los coches de transmisión automática o los de transmisión manual?
21. ¿Es posible que compres un coche este año?
22. Por lo general, ¿cuándo/con qué frecuencia usas tu coche?
23. ¿Dónde lo aparcas cuando vienes a la universidad? ¿Es difícil aparcar el coche en la universidad?

24. ¿Quién te enseñó a conducir? ¿Fue fácil o difícil para ti aprender a conducir?
25. Cuando conduces, ¿siempre respetas el límite de velocidad o vas muy rápido?

E. Definiciones. Use sentences like these as daily listening comprehension practice or for review.

1. Lo opuesto de "construir".
2. Un acto ilegal.
3. Lo opuesto de "abundancia".
4. Lo que hace John Wayne en gran parte de sus películas.
5. El lugar donde viven los pájaros.
6. El petróleo, los minerales y los árboles son todos ejemplos de __________.
7. El autobús y el tren son dos medios de __________.
8. El verbo sinónimo a "levantarse muy temprano".
9. Una persona que vive y trabaja en el campo.
10. Un tipo de edificio muy muy alto.
11. La electricidad es una forma de __________.
12. El lugar donde se produce algo: zapatos, botellas, autos.
13. Lo opuesto de "sucio" o "contaminado".
14. Cuando queda muy poco de un recurso natural, se dice que hay __________.

F. Cierto/Falso. These statements can be turned into **definiciones**, as well. Use them for daily listening practice, warm-up, or quiz questions.

1. Los coches grandes gastan poca gasolina.
2. Una autopista tiene más tráfico que un camino.
3. Un sinónimo de "aparcar" es "doblar".
4. No es necesario tomar un examen para obtener una licencia.
5. Se pone el aceite en el tanque.
6. Antes de hacer un viaje en coche, es buena idea revisar todo.
7. "Manejar" y "conducir" son sinónimos.
8. Es cierto que todos los mecánicos son honestos.
9. La gasolinera es la parte del coche en la que se pone la gasolina.
10. Algunos camiones tienen más de cuatro llantas.

G. ¿Indicativo, subjuntivo o pretérito? Have students listen as you read the following words. Point to students at random and have them tell you if the verb is conjugated in (present) indicative, (present) subjunctive, or preterite.

llegue	habló	paré
mire	choqué	mandé
buscó	estudie	llamé
practiqué	escuche	fumó
pagué	pregunte	practico
revisó	arregló	choque
revise	llene	llamo

III. GRAMMAR

The following worksheets are in the Student Supplement.

A. Past Participles and Present Perfect. (pp. 219-220) These worksheets practice indicative and subjunctive present perfect and formation of the past participle.

B. Una carta de España. (p. 221) This letter written by a Spanish woman shows "real-life" use of the present perfect. A cloze passage, followed by comprehension questions.

C. Repaso. (pp. 222-225)

NOTE: For more practice with the present perfect, have students do the translations below. Assign one sentence to each student to translate on the board, then review as a class.

Traducciones: En una fiesta

1. I've already had two beers. **(tomar)**
2. He's danced with her four times!
3. All the windows are open and the neighbors have complained.
4. It's incredible that the neighbors have called the police.
5. I can't believe that those guys have swum in the pool.
6. Have you asked for her phone number?
7. Yes. She hasn't given it to me...yet.
8. It's fantastic that my friends have returned with more food.
9. Oh, no! Those two girls gave fallen!
10. Yes, and now the lamp is broken.
11. I've never seen a party like this!
12. I hope that you've enjoyed yourself.
13. Thanks. I've really enjoyed myself.
14. I hope she's brought more music.
15. Me, too. I'm not tired yet.
16. Oh, no! Fred has fallen asleep in the bathtub!

IV. INTEGRATIVE ACTIVITIES

A. Charla. Chapter 14 offers a discussion topic students are almost certain to be interested in: the environment. You can begin the discussion using the listening passage about the environment in the Chapter 14 Teacher's Guide, and/or by looking over the words on p. 412 of *Puntos*. Students may want some extra words: **el vidrio**, **el cartón**, **ahorrar**, **la electricidad**, **orgánico**, **el reciclaje**, **la desforestación**, etc. Ask students if your city/area has environmental problems, and list their responses on the board, then discuss some country/world environmental problems. Once you've got a reasonable list of problems on the board, ask the students to offer solutions, and write down their ideas on the board. Continue the discussion by asking students what they do to help the environment. You can do this by asking questions like **¿Quién viene a la universidad en bicicleta? ¿Quién viene caminando? ¿Quién lleva cosas a un centro de reciclaje?**, etc. You could also have students in pairs tell each other what they do for the environment, and go over the findings with the whole class.

B. Entrevistas. Conversations between pairs of students give individual students more time to practice speaking. Distribute interview cards with the following three questions to students, or write the question on the board. Allow 2-3 minutes for students to interview each other, and ask several pairs to "perform" the interviews for the class.

Student 1 Ask your partner:

- what s/he has eaten today
- where s/he has gone today
- if s/he has talked with a friend today

Student 2 Ask your partner:

- what movie s/he has seen recently
- if s/he has done the homework
- if s/he has been to Mexico

C. Diálogos. See the two dialogue topics on p. 225 of the Student Supplement. Allow 4-5 minutes for students to create a conversation, then have pairs present their dialogues as time allows. Encourage students to use rough notes only and to improvise when possible. Ask the class to listen for errors and ask follow-up questions after each dialogue to check for comprehension. After presentation, review errors with the class.

D. Guided Writing: En una cantina cerca del Río Orinoco, Venezuela. On p. 226 of the Student Supplement you will find a drawing and accompanying questions. A good follow-up activity is to have students prepare a short, spontaneous dialogue between some of the characters in the drawing, using the vocabulary and grammar structures from Chapter 14. For example: Prepare a dialogue between Pepe and Juan in which they discuss what they've done and seen today. As a final activity, have students write a 100-word letter from one of the characters, describing what he/she has done on vacation in Venezuela.

E. Communicative Goals Practice #4. The picture and student guidelines are on p. 228 of the Student Supplement. Remember that these practices can be used individually, in pairs, or as a whole class. For an explanation of how to use these practices as preparation for oral interviews, see the Chapter 2 Teacher's Guide, p. 16.

V. GAMES

A. "Dame el nombre de..." This game is based on Exercise B on p. 420 of *Puntos*. Divide the class into two or more teams. Write the categories in Exercise B on slips of paper and put them in a bag or a hat. You may need some extra categories, such as **algo inventado en los EE.UU., un problema muy complicado, un libro leído por muchas personas, un lugar visitado por muchas personas, algo hecho de plástico.**

Have a student from the first team pick a slip of paper and read the category aloud, then name something that fits within that category: **"El teléfono es algo inventado en los EE.UU."** S/he then points to a member of the second team, who must also name something in that category. A team gets a point when the other team is unable to add another word to the category. Continue playing with new categories as long as students are interested.

B. "He bingado." This bingo practices with the present perfect. See p. 227 of the Student Supplement for the bingo card. You can do this as a follow-up to the pair interviews in INTEGRATIVE ACTIVITIES.

C. ¿Qué es? The purpose of this game is to get students to practice circumlocution. It requires planning one day in advance. First, for homework, have students think of five common household objects for which they don't know the Spanish words. Some examples are: *bookmark, flashlight, outlet, stapler, can opener*. Have students then write a simple definition in Spanish of the object in his/her own words. For example, for *bookmark*, an acceptable definition might be: **Es algo que usas cuando lees un libro. Pones esta cosa en la página del libro cuando no quieres leer más.** The next day, have students bring definitions to class and check them for comprehensibility only. Divide class into pairs and have students alternate defining things to each other and guessing the object defined. Give a prize to the pair that guesses the most objects correctly first. As a variation, you may also have students bring the objects they've defined to class. Divide the class into two teams, and instruct students to keep their objects hidden from the other team. Choose students to come to the front of the room and face away from the class. Have a student from Team A read a definition to the student from Team B at the front of the class, while holding up the object defined so everyone else can see it. Team B gets a point if the member correctly guesses the object. Then a student from Team A comes to the front of the class, and so on.

CAPÍTULO 15

Communicative Goals for Chapter 15
By the end of the chapter students should be able to:

* talk about sentimental relationships	☐
* discuss the different stages of life	☐
* describe their ideal companion, friend, job, apartment, vacation spot, etc.	☐
* discuss cause-and-effect relationships	☐

Grammatical Structures
Students should know:

* subjunctive after nonexistent and indefinite antecedents	☐
* subjunctive after conjunctions of contingency and purpose	☐

I. PRONUNCIATION

A. Use the dialogue on p. 446 of *Puntos* for pronunciation and intonation practice. Read the conversation once at close-to-normal speed while students listen and repeat, reading along in their texts. Then repeat the dialogue at a faster speed and ask students to repeat. Students enjoy being able to say full Spanish sentences quickly. Stress intonation and the linking of vowels at the ends and beginnings of words:

--¿Tenéis planes par<u>a e</u>sta noche?
--Creo que no, a menos que Manol<u>o</u> <u>hay</u><u>a</u> <u>he</u>cho planes.

Have students break into pairs to practice the dialogue, reading alternate lines to each other. You can also ask students to practice the dialogue in pairs outside of class and perform it in class the next day.

B. See the "frases locas" on p. 229 of the Student Supplement for another pronunciation practice.

II. LISTENING COMPREHENSION

A. <u>En casa de Miguel</u>. Read the following script of a conversation between two friends about what their housemates are doing. Students listen to the conversation and compete the answer sheet on p. 229 of the Student Supplement.

INSTRUCTIONS (read to students):

Miguel and Roque live in a co-op with some other Hispanic students. One afternoon Miguel returns home to find the house is empty except for Roque. Listen to their conversation about what everyone else is doing. I'll read both parts. The first time you hear the passage, number the activities below in the order you hear them mentioned and match each activity with the person(s) doing it. The second time you hear the conversation, listen for the answers to the questions below.

M: Hola, todos... ¿Hola?... ¿Rosa? ¿Víctor? ¿Carmen? ¿Sancho? ¿Roque? ¿Marta?
R: Hola, Miguel. Ven aquí. Estoy en la cocina.
(Miguel entra en la cocina.)
M: ¿Qué pasa por aquí? ¿Dónde está todo el mundo?
R: Pues, déjame pensar... Víctor fue al cine para ver esa nueva película de Woody Allen.

M: ¡Caramba! Yo quería ver esa película con él. ¿Y Marta? ¿Fue también?
R: No, ella no. Una amiga acaba de buscarla. Las dos iban a jugar tenis.
M: Ah, claro. Casi se me olvida. Hoy es la competencia entre nuestra casa y el Club Latino, ¿no?
R: Sí, hombre. Rosa y Sancho fueron a verlas jugar unos partidos, y creo que hicieron planes para ir a nadar al lago después.
M: ¿Y Carmen?
R: Pues, a estas horas ya debe estar en la galería. Esta noche empieza la exposición de sus fotos, ¿no te acuerdas?
M: Ah, sí, sí. Bueno...y tú, ¿qué planes tienes?
R: Ninguno en particular. Estoy un poco cansado. Iba a comer algo y después sentarme en el patio a tomar un poco del sol. ¿Me acompañas?
M: Sí, con mucho gusto. ¡Vamos!

B. Preguntas personales. Use these are warm-up, discussion questions, or as daily listening comprehension practice.

1. ¿Tienes un(a) mejor amigo/a)? ¿Cómo es esa persona?
2. ¿Te consideras un buen amigo/buena amiga?
3. Para ti, ¿cuál es más importante: la amistad, el amor, la familia, la salud...? ¿Por qué?
4. ¿Crees que el amor verdadero existe?
5. ¿Has estado enamorado/a alguna vez? ¿Estás enamorado/a ahora?
6. ¿Cuáles son las características de una pareja ideal?
7. ¿Qué te gusta hacer cuando sales con tus amigos?
8. ¿Con quién pasas la mayoría de tu tiempo?
9. ¿Qué te gusta hacer en una cita?
10. Para ti, ¿cómo sería la luna de miel más romántica?
11. ¿Cuál es la mejor manera de invitar a alguien a salir?
12. ¿Cuál es la mejor manera de romper con alguien?
13. ¿Dónde naciste?

C. Definiciones. You read the definitions to the class while they listen and supply the correct word. Here are some possible definitions from Chapter 15.

1. La relación sentimental y fuerte que existe entre personas que se quieren mucho.
2. El período de tiempo, a veces largo y a veces corto, por el que los novios pasan antes del matrimonio.
3. Una actividad que hacen juntos los amigos, los novios, etc. Un ejemplo es ir al cine y después a comer algo.
4. La relación que existe entre los amigos.
5. El resultado de un matrimonio infeliz o desastroso; después de obtener esta cosa, el hombre y la mujer ya no viven juntos.
6. Una ceremonia, religiosa o civil, en que el novio y la novia se hacen esposo y esposa. A veces asisten parientes y amigos y la novia lleva un vestido blanco.
7. Lo opuesto de nacer.
8. La etapa de la vida entre la infancia y la adolescencia.
9. Algo que hacen los niños y las plantas.
10. Lo opuesto de juventud.

III. GRAMMAR

The following worksheets and practice sheets are in the Student Supplement.

A. Subjunctive in adjective clauses. (pp. 230-231) Before having students do these worksheets, present this usage of the subjunctive. Begin by writing on the board **Busco un/a novio/a** and adding several completions: **que sea sincero/a, que sepa comprenderme, que me tenga confianza**, etc. If the above example doesn't apply to you, try **Busco una casa / un coche / un gato**, etc. Then ask students to add other completions on the board, changing the verbs to subjunctive as necessary. After you've listed 4-5 completions, ask students to find and explain the pattern. Read through the explanation on pp. 439-440 of *Puntos* if students are still having trouble. Then put a new topic on the board: **Busco un trabajo que...** Ask students to write down 2-3 completions to the sentence about their ideal job after graduation. Give students a few minutes to do this, then call on some of them to describe what sort of job they're looking for. to the rest of the class. Then assign the worksheet on p. 231 of the Student Supplement for homework or as an in-class practice. Try to compile responses and form a consensus about students' ideal jobs, homes, etc.

B. ¿Hay alguien aquí que...? (p. 232) This art-based practice is a good follow-up activity for subjunctive in adjective clauses.

C. Subjunctive vs. indicative. (p. 233) This worksheet practices the distinction between definite and indefinite/nonexisting antecedents.

D. Subjunctive after certain conjunctions. (p. 234) This writing activity practices subjunctive with **antes (de) que**, **para que**, **a menos que**, **con tal (de) que**, and **en caso de que**.

E. Subjunctive of contingency and purpose. (pp. 235-236) An art-based, two-page writing practice.

F. Subjunctive, Indicative or Infinitive? (p. 237) This cloze passage incorporates all uses of subjunctive presented so far. A good review practice.

G. Repaso. (pp. 238-240)

IV. INTEGRATIVE ACTIVITIES

A. Entrevistas. Conversations between pairs of students give individual students more time to practice speaking. Distribute interview cards with the following questions to students, or write the questions on the board. Allow 4-5 minutes for students to interview each other, and ask several pairs to "perform" their interviews for the class.

Student 1 - Ask your partner:	Student 2 - Ask your partner:
1. If s/he had a date last weekend.	1. Where s/he was born.
2. What his/her best friend is like.	2. Where s/he would like to go on a honeymoon.
3. If s/he is in love.	3. If s/he has a date this weekend.

B. Carta/Guía. Tell students that Irina, an Uruguayan exchange student, will be spending next semester in (*your town*) and needs some information. Have students, working as a whole class, write a letter to Irina, including the following details: what to look forward to, what to avoid, special cultural and athletic events, where to go to "get away from it all," what to do to spend a little/a lot of money, where to go for good food, how to meet people, what classes to take, what to do in her spare time. Have one student at the board write the letter as others make suggestions. Help out with structures and vocabulary as needed and encourage students to use subjunctive and informal commands. Remind them of the phrases used to begin and end letters. When the letter is complete, review it with students, asking them to point out mistakes and to add other suggestions. Call on several students to read pieces of the letter aloud.

C. Guided Writing: En la playa. See p. 241 of the Student Supplement for picture and accompanying questions. A good follow-up activity is to have students prepare short spontaneous dialogues between some of the characters in the drawing using the vocabulary from Chapter 15. For example: Prepare a dialogue between Susana and Miguel in which they make plans for their wedding. You might also have students write a 100-word letter from one of the characters, again incorporating Chapter 15 vocabulary and structures.

V. GAMES

A. Bingo: Capítulo 15. See Student Supplement, p. 242.

CAPÍTULO 16

Communicative Goals for Chapter 16
By the end of the chapter students should be able to:

* discuss careers and money matters	☐
* talk about the future	☐
* talk about pending actions	☐
* express conjecture	☐

Grammatical Structures
Students should know:

* future verb forms	☐
* subjunctive and indicative after conjunctions of time	☐

I. PRONUNCIATION

Read the sentences below to students, then have them practice with a partner, using the sheet on p. 243 of the Student Supplement. Tell students to pay attention to the accents on future verb forms.

- Cuando Carlota pueda, pedirá un préstamo, comprará un coche y lo pagará a plazos.
- Los señores Suárez visitarán Acapulco, donde alquilarán una habitación en el Hotel Regina.
- Paquita Palacios tomará un taxi al centro de Puebla, y pagará tres mil pesos.
- En veinticinco años, tendremos una mujer presidente, colonizaremos la luna, eliminaremos las armas nucleares y seremos todos bilingües.

II. LISTENING COMPREHENSION

A. ¿A cuánto está el cambio? This is a good opportunity to review numbers again. Have students fill in the chart on p. 243 of the Student Supplement as you dictate the foreign exchange rates for the day. Then have them calculate a few problems using this information and the future tense.

For example: Hoy en Argentina un dólar estadounidense equivale a .99 pesos.

Argentina	.99	pesos
Chile	416	pesos
Colombia	1056	pesos
Ecuador	3822	sucres
México	7.86	nuevos pesos
España	144	pesetas
Uruguay	9.19	nuevos pesos
Venezuela	480	bolívares

1. Si cambias 150 dólares en Buenos Aires, ¿cuántos pesos recibirás?
2. Si cambias 200 dólares en Madrid, ¿cuántas pesetas recibirás?
3. Si cambias 1000 dólares en Cancún, ¿cuántos nuevos pesos recibirás?
4. Si cambias 500 dólares en Quito, ¿cuántos sucres recibirás?

B. Los salarios de mis amigos. Have students listen as you read them some of your friends' salaries and professions. They should fill in the chart on p. 243 of the Student Supplement. When they are finished, you can check to see if they got the salaries right by asking them to list the names of your friends in order from highest to lowest.

1. Roberto, el que me ayuda a cobrar cheques en el Banco Nacional, gana $18.000 al año.
2. Raúl Méndez, el que me curó cuando estaba enfermo/a, gana $120.000 al año.
3. Martín, el que me corta el pelo, gana $22.000 al año.
4. Margarita, la que reparó mi horno y mis lámparas la semana pasada, gana $32.000 al año.
5. Lorenzo, el que le enseña matemáticas a mi hijo, gana $28.000 al año.
6. Mari Carmen, la que me ayudó con los seguros cuando tuve mi accidente, gana $150.000 al año.
7. Rafa, el que trabaja en la biblioteca de nuestro barrio, gana $20.000 al año.
8. José Carlos, el que nos salvó cuando nuestra tubería estaba rota y había agua por toda la casa, gana $75.000 al año.
9. Rosalía, la que trabaja en el departamento de carreteras para la ciudad de San Diego, gana $85.000 al año.

C. Definiciones. Good for warm-up or quick listening comprehension checks. Have students keep their texts open to p. 460 during definitions 11 through 20.

1. Lo que tienes que pagar todos los meses para mantener los servicios de gas, luz, teléfono, etcétera
2. Lo opuesto de "gastar mucho."
3. El dinero que alguien te presta.
4. Lo opuesto de "sacar dinero."
5. Lo que debes hacer con tu cuenta corriente todos los meses si quieres saber cuánto dinero tienes.
6. Si necesitas dinero a las once de la noche, puedes ir a un:
7. Acción de ir pagando algo poco a poco:
8. El librito donde guardas los cheques:
9. Si estás en un restaurante donde no se aceptan ni cheques ni tarjetas de crédito, ¿cómo vas a pagar?
10. Un plan que explica en qué vas a gastar tu dinero, cómo vas a economizar, etc.:
11. Persona que prepara las comidas en un restaurante.
12. Persona que trabaja con las computadoras.
13. Persona que ayuda a curar a los animales enfermos.
14. Persona que arregla los coches.
15. Persona que diseña carreteras, puentes, etc.
16. Persona que sabe hablar y escribir más de un idioma.
17. Persona que trabaja con números.
18. Persona que trabaja en las fuerzas armadas.
19. Persona que enseña a los niños de la escuela secundaria.
20. Persona que trabaja en la casa de otro, ayudando con la limpieza.

D. Dictado. Remember to dictate in "chunks" of a few words, then tell the students how many words are in each sentence. Repeat the sentence once and correct immediately. This dictation is good to see if students are hearing the use of the subjunctive after conjunctions of time; it also includes a lot of new vocabulary. These sentences are from p. 474 of *Puntos*.

1. Rigoberto se va a comprar / una computadora / en cuanto el banco / le dé el préstamo. (15)
2. Siempre usa su tarjeta de crédito / cuando no tiene / dinero en efectivo. (12)
3. Cada mes balancea su cuenta corriente / después de que el banco / le envía su estado de cuentas. (17)
4. Piensa abrir una cuenta de ahorros / tan pronto como consiga un trabajo. (12)
5. No puede pagar sus cuentas este mes / hasta que su hermano / le devuelva el dinero / que le prestó. (18)

E. Preguntas personales. We've included two sets of questions, the first dealing with Chapter 16 vocabulary and the second practicing new chapter structures.

1. ¿Qué haces cuando necesitas dinero?
2. ¿Pagas las facturas cuando llegan, o esperas un poquito?
3. ¿Sabes balancear tu cuenta corriente?
4. Cuando compras algo, ¿cómo prefieres pagar?
5. ¿A veces les pides un préstamo a tus padres o a tus amigos?
6. ¿Alguna vez le has prestado dinero a alguien?
7. Para ti, ¿es fácil o difícil ahorrar dinero?
8. ¿Cuáles son tus gastos mayores?
9. ¿Tienes una tarjeta de crédito? ¿La usas mucho?
10. ¿Pagas el alquiler tú solo/a o tus padres te ayudan a pagarlo?
11. Cuando tenías 10 años, ¿qué profesión querías tener?
12. Cuando te gradúes, ¿qué tipo de trabajo vas a buscar?
13. ¿Cuál es una de las profesiones más prestigiosas en tu opinión? ¿Por qué?
14. ¿Cuáles son unos de los trabajos que has tenido durante tus años universitarios?
15. ¿Cuál es la carrera ideal para tu mejor amigo/a? ¿Por qué?
16. ¿Cómo te sientes cuando tienes una entrevista?
17. ¿Has tenido una entrevista terrible alguna vez?
18. ¿Has tenido un/a jefe/a muy malo/a en un trabajo? ¿Cómo era? ¿Qué hacía?
19. En tu opinión, ¿ser siquiatra es buena profesión? ¿Por qué sí? ¿Por qué no?
20. ¿Es justo que los plomeros ganen más dinero que los maestros? ¿Por qué?

Cuando te gradúes...

1. ¿Dónde vivirás?
2. ¿Qué tipo de trabajo buscarás?
3. ¿Recibirás un regalo especial?
4. ¿Estarás contento/a o triste? ¿Por qué?

En el año 2020...

5. ¿Qué tipo de ayuda doméstica tendremos?
6. ¿Cómo cambiarán los aviones?
7. ¿Cuánto dinero costará una casa en San Francisco?
8. ¿Adónde viajaremos para las vacaciones?

Cuando tengas una familia...

9. ¿Serás muy estricto/a?
10. ¿Tendrás más de dos hijos?

11. ¿Qué nombres les pondrás?
12. ¿A qué universidad asistirán tus hijos?

F. Multiple-choice. These statements are great for review or quizzes.

1. Si tienes un problema legal, debes consultar con un: a) abogado, b) carpintero, c) pintor.
2. Si te interesa mucho la política, una buena carrera para ti sería la de: a) siquiatra, b) comerciante, c) senador.
3. ¡Uff! Me duele mucho una muela. Voy a llamar al: a) detective, b) dentista, c) dependiente.
4. Casi llega el 15 de abril y necesitas pagar los impuestos. ¿Quién te puede ayudar? a) una cantante, b) una contadora, c) una comerciante.
5. Necesitas hacer un informe para tu clase de historia pero no sabes dónde están los libros. ¿Con quién vas a hablar? a) la fotógrafa, b) la bibliotecaria, c) la médica.
6. Pensabas graduarte este semestre, ¡pero acabas de saber que todavía te faltan 10 créditos! Debes ir ahora mismo a la oficina del: a) rabino, b) consejero, c) policía.
7. ¡Por Dios! Tu microondas acaba de explotar y ninguna de las lámparas de tu casa funciona. Es buena idea llamar a una: a) abogada, b) plomero, c) electricista.
8. Es el final del semestre. Tienes muchos problemas emocionales por las presiones que sufres. Necesitas hablar con un: a) psicólogo, b) traductor, c) periodista.
9. Tu pelo está hecho un desastre y te ves horrible. Para un corte de pelo nuevo, hay que ir a la: a) siquiatra, b) peluquera, c) mecánica.
10. Necesitas un trabajo a plazo medio para pagar la matrícula y el alquiler. Puedes buscar trabajo en un restaurante como: a) camarero, b) criado, c) carpintero.

III. GRAMMAR

The following worksheets are in the Student Supplement.

A. Translation Drill. (p. 245) Chapter 16 is a good time for students to review all the verb forms presented up to this point.

B. El futuro. (p. 246) Three short cloze passages.

C. Los empleados del Banco Mundial. (p. 247) This art-based worksheet focuses on making conjectures with future forms.

D. Conjunctions of Time: Lo malo de ganar un buen sueldo. (p. 248) A three-part worksheet. This is a good introductory practice for subjunctive with conjunctions of time.

E. Subjunctive vs. Indicative after Conjunctions of Time. (p. 249) This art-based worksheet contains three short cloze passages.

F. Cuando yo sea grande... (p. 250) Another art-based activity, combining Chapter 16 vocabulary, future forms, and subjunctive with conjunctions of time.

G. Repaso. (pp. 251-254)

IV. INTEGRATIVE ACTIVITIES

A. Diálogos: Capítulo 16. See dialogue ideas on p. 255 of the Student Supplement.

B. Especulaciones. Bring in odd or interesting magazine picture of people and use them to elicit responses using future of conjecture. You ask questions such as **¿Dónde estarán? ¿Quién será? ¿Cuántos años tendrá? ¿Cuánto dinero ganará?** Encourage students to come up with humorous or improbable guesses. You can even ask students to bring in funny pictures from magazines which you can then add to your picture file.

C. Entrevistas. Give pairs of students 2-3 minutes to conduct the interviews, then call on a few pairs of students to perform them for the class.

Partner A - ask your partner:
- where s/he will live in the year 2000
- if s/he has a budget
- if s/he can lend you $10

Partner B - ask your partner:
- what job s/he will have in the year 2000
- if s/he balances his/her checking account
- if s/he pays the bills on time

D. Information Gap Activity: Los préstamos del Banco Exterior de Miami. This activity practices with large numbers. See p. 257 of the Student Supplement for the chart and instructions. Divide the class into pairs and allow students 4-6 minutes to fill in the charts. Remind partners not to look at each other's charts. Afterward, discuss as a class who should get a loan and why.

E. Guided Writing: De compras. See p. 258 of the Student Supplement for the picture and questions. Follow up by having students present short, spontaneous dialogues between any two characters in the drawing. You might also have them write a 100-word letter from one of the characters, using Chapter 16 vocabulary and structures.

V. GAMES

A. Bingaré. This version of Bingo (Student Supplement, p. 256) practices with the future verb forms.

B. El futuro de la clase de español. If your students know each other fairly well, this is a fun listening comprehension and guessing game. First, on slips of paper, have each student write 2-3 sentences saying what s/he will be doing and where s/he will be working and living in the year 2010, and sign the papers. Collect all the slips and divide the class into two teams. Read the first "prediction" slip to the teams without saying who wrote it. Ask the teams: **¿Quién será?** The team that guesses the identity of the person wins a point. Obviously, students are not allowed to use their own predictions. Read half of the predictions in one game and save the others for another day.

C. Charades. If you have an extroverted class, have students act out the different professions and occupations in teams.

CAPÍTULO 17

Communicative Goals for Chapter 17
By the end of the chapter students should be able to:

* discuss current events ☐
* express doubts, emotions, and wishes in the past ☐
* talk about what belongs to them and others ☐

Grammatical Structures
Students should know:

* past subjunctive ☐
* stressed possessives ☐

I. PRONUNCIATION

Read the sentences below to students and ask them to repeat. Then have students practice with a partner, referring to p. 259 of the Student Supplement.

- Daniel Durán dudaba que durara el desastre de la dictadura.
- Susana Sánchez sintió que el senador no supiera representar a los ciudadanos satsfactoriamente.
- Tomás Torres temía que el testigo no tomara en serio la tragedia del terremoto.
- El reportero recomendó que Rubén Ruíz regresara a Rusia rápidamente.
- Héctor Hernández hizo que Herlinda Haros invitara a su hermano a la huelga.

II. LISTENING COMPREHENSION

A. News Report. Below is a sample news report to read to students. They should refer to the chart on p. 259 of the Student Supplement.

INSTRUCTIONS (read to students):

You will hear a news report. The first time you hear it, listen for who is being talked about and where the event took place. Write this information in the chart below. The second time you hear the report, complete the chart with information about what happened. Don't worry about understanding everything you hear.

Buenas noches a todos. El Canal 11 les ofrece el noticiero de las seis, con nuestra reportera Sonia Suárez. ¿Sonia?

Gracias, y buenas noches. El acontecimiento más notable del día fue el viaje del presidente estadounidense a Berlín, Alemania. Allí el Presidente se va a reunir con otros líderes europeos, entre ellos el Presidente de Francia, el Presidente de España y el Primer Ministro de Inglaterra. En esta reunión se va a hablar de dos temas: primero, el acuerdo económico entre la Comunidad Europea y los Estados Unidos; segundo, la guerra en Bosnia-Hersegovina.

En Londres, se murió la Reina Elizabeth II en un choque automovilístico. La familia real inglesa anunció hoy que el Príncipe de Gales, Carlos, será nombrado Rey el lunes. El Parlamento inglés declaró tres días de luto oficial. También en Londres, explotó otra bomba en el metro, matando a dos personas y haciendo que el sistema de metro se cerrara por cuatro horas. La policía londinense declaró que fue otro ataque del Ejército de la República de Irlanda.

En Sicilia, Italia, la erupción volcánica de ayer ha sido la causa de la muerte de más de 40 personas. Según la Cruz Roja, que empezó ayer sus esfuerzos de atención médica, todavía quedan muchas personas por rescatar.

B. Dictado. Dictations are especially helpful at this point, especially as students are getting used to the new past subjunctive forms. Don't forget to dictate in "chunks" of a few words at a time.

1. Mis amigos me recomendaron que / viviera en una residencia universitaria / en vez de un apartamento. (15)
2. Te digo de verdad / que nunca creí / que hubiera alguien / que apoyara a ese candidato. (15)
3. Era necesario / que mi padre tuviera dos trabajos / para que yo pudiera asistir / a la universidad. (16)
4. Hace treinta años, / era difícil que Jorge y Juan / hablaran de las elecciones / sin pelearse. (15)
5. Era necesario / que volviéramos a casa / a una hora determinada, / aun los fines de semana. (15)

C. Discrimination Drill (I). Read the following sentences to students and have them write "Present" or "Past" after they hear each sentence.

1. Supimos de los planes de los obreros al llegar a la oficina.
2. Mi jefe quería que su secretaria terminara antes de la manifestación.
3. Enrique viene para enterarse de las causas de la huelga.
4. Todo el mundo espera que la huelga termine pronto.
5. Marta no quería que su esposo participara.
6. Los obreros esperan recibir un aumento de sueldo.
7. Era necesario que la policía viniera a las seis de la tarde.
8. Gracias a Dios, todo salió sin problemas.

D. Discrimination Drill (II). This is intended to help students distinguish between preterite and past subjunctive.

INSTRUCTIONS (read to students):

You will hear some sentences about the past. If the sentence simply narrates what happened, write "I" (indicative) on your paper. If the sentence expresses a wish, doubt, or emotion about the past event, write "S" (subjunctive) on your paper.

1. Esperabas que vinieras a visitarme.
2. Terminaron a las ocho y media.
3. Quería que lo hiciera pronto.
4. Me dieron dos regalos maravillosos.
5. Nos pidió que pagáramos al contado.
6. Temía que no quisiera ir.
7. Estuvieron en Sevilla dos semanas.
8. Era una lástima que estuvieran enfermos.
9. Les explicaron el problema ayer.
10. Dudaba que pudiéramos ayudar.

11. No creía que nadie supiera la verdad.
12. Compraron un coche alemán.
13. Era increíble que costara tanto.

E. Preguntas personales.

1. ¿Cómo te enteras de las noticias?
2. ¿Cuántas horas al día ves televisión, más o menos?
3. ¿Quién es tu reportero/a favorito/a? ¿Por qué?
4. ¿Te gusta ver el noticiero? ¿Por qué?
5. Hoy en día, ¿qué país extranjero sale más frecuentemente en las noticias?
6. ¿Te gustan los programas de entrevistas, como *Geraldo* y *Oprah*? ¿Por qué?
7. ¿Viste la televisión anoche?
8. ¿Qué programas viste?
9. Después del noticiero, ¿te gusta ver los programas de David Letterman o Jay Leno?
10. ¿Quién es más cómico en tu opinión?
11. ¿Te gusta que haya programas como "911" y "Cops"? ¿Por qué?
12. ¿Has visto un programa excelente en la tele recientemente? ¿Cuál?
13. ¿Cuál es un acontecimiento que te ha afectado profundamente?
14. Cuando eras joven, ¿veías la tele mientras cenabas con tu familia?
15. ¿Te gusta ver deportes en la tele?
16. ¿Recibes algún periódico o alguna revista en casa? ¿Cuál?
17. ¿Qué opinas del periódico de esta ciudad?
18. ¿Lees el periódico todos los días?
19. ¿Qué sección del periódico te gusta más? ¿Por qué?
20. ¿Te interesa la política o te parece aburrida?
21. ¿Qué opinas del Presidente Clinton?
22. Para ti, ¿cuál es el derecho humano más importante?
23. ¿Crees que el servicio militar debe ser un deber de todos los ciudadanos?

III. GRAMMAR

The following worksheets are in the Student Supplement.

A. Titulares. (p. 260) This practice asks students to react to fictitious headlines using the subjunctive. It may be done as an in-class pair activity.

B. El imperfecto del subjuntivo. (pp. 261-262) These worksheets, both sentence completions, practice new imperfect subjunctive forms.

C. Párrafos cortos: El imperfecto del subjuntivo. (p. 263) An art-based writing assignment. You can give this as homework and do group compositions in class the next day.

D. Ojalá que... (p. 263) Students create a "wish list" using **ojalá** + past subjunctive. Follow up by having students compare wishes in class.

F. Stressed Possessives. (p. 265) A cloze passage.

G. Repaso. (pp. 266-269)

IV. INTEGRATIVE ACTIVITIES

A. El noticiero de la clase. Divide students into groups of three or four and have them prepare a short (3 minutes maximum) "broadcast" to present to the class. Have each member of the group be responsible for one or more of the following categories:

- national and international news
- local news
- weather
- sports
- entertainment

If your area has access to Univisión or Telemundo news broadcasts, have students watch the news to help prepare for their presentations.

B. Entrevistas. These quick pair interviews are a good way to get the whole class to practice listening and speaking. Put the questions up on the board and allow about 1-2 minutes for the interviews. Call on several pairs of students to do their interviews to the class. You may want to model an interview before starting the activity.

Partner A - Ask your partner:
- if s/he watched the news last night.
- if s/he always obeys the law.
- if s/he has ever been in a car crash.

Partner B - Ask your partner:
- if s/he voted in the last elections.
- what paper s/he reads.
- if s/he has ever been in an earthquake.

C. Guided Writing: Las noticias desde Chicago, 1925. See p. 270 of the Student Supplement for drawing and accompanying questions.

V. GAMES

A. Verb competition. Here are 2 versions of the game, one quick and easy and the other a bit more timeconsuming for the teacher, but more exciting for the students.

1. "Flashcards." Make 15-20 flashcards with common infinitives written on them. Divide the class into 2 teams, and have each team line up on either side of the class. Show the infinitive to the teams and call out a person and tense/mood for the verb. For example, if the verb is **salir**, say "yo, present subjunctive." Try to work in a variety of tenses and moods: imperfect, preterite, present perfect, present subjunctive, future, past subjunctive. The first student in each team's line goes up to the board and writes the form. The student who correctly writes the form first gets a point for the team, an then both students sit down. The team with the most points at the end wins. This game works well around the third or fourth day of the chapter, when students have had some practice with the new forms.

2. "Relay Race." The night before you play the game, make 4 identical sets of flashcards. On each card, write a verb infinitive, a person, and a tense/mood. For example: "salir, yo, present subjunctive." Try to cover a variety of tenses and moods: imperfect, preterite, present perfect, present subjunctive, past subjunctive. Divide the class into 4 teams and have each team sit in a row if possible. Give the top flashcard to the first student in each row/team, and make a signal for them to go to the board and write the form. After they write, they return to their seats, and the next student down gets a

new card, and so forth. Each team member is allowed to correct anything his/her members have written previously. Try to do this game on two separate chalkboards to discourage teams from looking at each others' answers. At the time limit you've set, signal the students to sit down. Review each team's answers with the class. The team with the greatest number of correct answers wins.

CAPÍTULO 18

Communicative Goals for Chapter 18
By the end of the chapter students should be able to:

* discuss travel plans and where to stay	☐
* hypothesize	☐
* talk about what they would do in certain situations	☐

Grammatical Structures
Students should know:

* conditional verb forms	☐
* if clauses	☐

I. PRONUNCIATION

Read the following sentences and have students repeat. Then have them practice in pairs. These sentences are on p. 271 of the Student Supplement.

- Paco Padilla no pudo encontrar su pasaporte porque lo había puesto en sus pantalones pardos que dejó en la pensión en Pamplona.
- Ana Amaral admitió que la azafata anunció algo acerca de la aduana, pero no lo escuchó.
- Tito Tamarindo temía que todos los turistas tomaran el tren a Toledo en vez de ir a Tarragona.
- Héctor y Herlinda han sido huéspedes en el humilde Hotel Holanda por ocho días, pero ahora han hecho una reserva en un hotel más hermoso.

II. LISTENING COMPREHENSION

A. ¿Dónde están? Students complete the answer sheet on p. 271 of the Student Supplement as you read excerpts from several conversations. Do this after presenting the new Chapter 18 vocabulary.

INSTRUCTIONS (read to students):

You will hear parts of several conversations taking place in Madrid. As you listen to each speaker, decide where s/he is, and circle the corresponding place from the choices on your answer sheet.

1. ¿Nos trae un café con leche doble y un agua mineral, por favor?
2. Buenas tardes. Quisiera mandar este paquete a los EE.UU.
3. Buenos días. Dos paquetes de fósforos, por favor. Y me da también 10 sellos de 55 pesetas.
4. Buenas tardes. Por favor, ¿me podría dar esta receta? Y también necesito curitas, aspirinas y algo para una tos seca.
5. ¿Qué prefieres merendar? ¿Pastel de chocolate o tarta de manzana? ¿O tal vez una empanada?
6. Entramos aquí un momento, ¿quieres? Me hace falta comprar un cuaderno y unos sobres.
7. Buenos días. ¿Tiene Ud. revistas en francés? ¿No? Entonces, me da *El País* y el último número de *Hola*, por favor. Y estas dos postales, también.

8. Me parece que tenemos que bajarnos en la próxima estación, y luego cambiar a la línea amarilla para ir a la Puerta del Sol.
9. Perdone Ud. ¿Lleva mucho tiempo esperando? ¿Podría decirme si ya pasó el bus número 44?
10. Esas 2 maletas son mías -- la azul y la negra. Y aquí tiene Ud. mi pasaporte.
11. Buenas noches. Quisiera una habitación doble con baño privado, por favor.

B. Definiciones. These are good for warm-up or quick listening comprehension checks.

1. La persona que nos ayuda con el equipaje.
2. El dinero que pagamos al inspector de la aduana si hemos comprado más de lo que se permite.
3. La persona que se aloja en un hotel o en una pensión.
4. Un hotel de primera categoría.
5. Lo que necesitas para lavarte el pelo.
6. El documento oficial que indica nuestra nacionalidad.
7. Si fumas, entonces usas muchos de éstos.
8. Dos cosas que necesitas para mandar una carta.
9. Una bebida muy rica hecha de frutas, helado o leche, que se sirve fría.
10. Palabra que se usa para describir un hotel sin habitaciones desocupadas.

C. Cierto/Falso

1. Si no declaras todas tus compras, el inspector de la aduana puede ponerte una multa.
2. Es buena idea ofrecerle al inspector una propina grande para que no registre tus maletas.
3. Es muy barato alojarse en un hotel de lujo en Madrid o Barcelona.
4. Un mozo espera recibir una propina si te ayuda con el equipaje.
5. Si haces una reserva en una pensión con pensión completa, quiere decir que el desayuno y una comida más están incluidas.

D. Preguntas personales. We've included questions for this chapter practicing with the new vocabulary and the chapter grammar (imperfect subjunctive and conditional).

1. ¿Has viajado al extranjero? ¿Adónde?
2. ¿Fuiste a México durante las vacaciones de primavera alguna vez? ¿Qué tal?
3. ¿Has tenido una experiencia negativa en la aduana? Explica.
4. ¿Qué recomiendas que un/a compañero/a haga para no tener problemas en la aduana?
5. ¿Cuáles son las ventajas de alojarse en un pensión en vez de en un hotel?
6. Si tuvieras suficiente dinero, ¿adónde viajarías? ¿Por qué?
7. Si estuvieras en España, ¿preferirías alquilar un coche o viajar por tren?
8. En general, ¿cómo prefieres viajar, por avión o por tren?
9. Si tus padres te visitaran, ¿adónde irían Uds. para cenar?
10. Si tuvieras que comprarle un regalo a un amigo, ¿dónde irías?
11. ¿Te gustaría trabajar en un hotel?
12. ¿Pasarías un año en un país hispano, si tuvieras la oportunidad? ¿Por qué?

If your students are having a hard time catching on to the combination of conditional and past subjunctive, you may want to have students answer these questions as a written homework assignment first, then review answers orally in class. Here are some questions specifically practicing imperfect subjunctive with conditional:

Si tuvieras un millón de dólares...

1. ¿Qué harías primero?
2. ¿Continuarías como estudiante o cambiarías tu vida?
3. ¿Harías algo por tu familia o tus amigos?
4. ¿Adónde viajarías?
5. ¿Qué comprarías?

Si pudieras tener tu casa ideal...

1. ¿Cómo sería?
2. ¿Dónde estaría?
3. ¿Quién viviría contigo allí?
4. ¿Qué harías allí?

Si tuvieras poderes mágicos y si pudieras cambiar cualquier cosa...

1. ¿Cómo cambiarías tu propia vida?
2. ¿Harías algún cambio en la vida de algún pariente o amigo?
3. ¿Estarías más feliz?
4. ¿Harías algo para cambiar algún problema nacional o internacional?

E. Dictado

1. Si pudiéramos conseguir un buen puesto, / ganaríamos bastante dinero / para comprar un coche nuevo. (14)
2. Si tuviera sed en este momento, / tomaría un vaso de agua fría. (12)
3. Si los estudiantes fueran profesores / y los profesores fueran estudiantes, / sería un cambio interesante. (15)
4. La mañana de la entrevista, / Ud. se levantó temprano, / se vistió con cuidado / y salió temprano para llegar puntualmente. (19)
5. Cucho Cano, el cocinero de Cádiz, / cocinará calamares calientes / con una copa de champán, / pero no puede contar / con la calidad del champán. (23)

III. GRAMMAR

The following worksheets are all in the Student Supplement.

A. El condicional. (p. 272) Two short cloze passages practicing with conditional forms. A good practice for early in the chapter before combining conditional with past subjunctive.

B. ¿Qué harías? (p. 273) An art-based activity that works with imperfect subjunctive and conditional in a controlled situation. Students' answers to the questions can be funny; you may want to assign this as a written homework activity and do an oral review in class the next day.

C. Planeando un viaje. (p. 274) Another art-based activity, practicing the conditional and new Chapter 18 vocabulary.

D. Práctica: El condicional y el imperfecto del subjuntivo. (p. 275) This worksheet has students complete personalized statements about "what would happen if . . ." A good follow-up activity is to pick several of the statements that would interest your students most and lead a class discussion on different student responses.

E. Práctica: Si yo fuera... (p. 276) Another fun, art-based worksheet practicing conditional with imperfect subjunctive.

F. ¡Problemas, problemas! (p. 277) Students give advice using imperfect subjunctive and conditional.

G. Repaso. (pp. 278-280)

IV. INTEGRATIVE ACTIVITIES

A. Si estuviera... Assign each student a city in a Spanish-speaking country. They should research five facts about their city. Each day have 5-6 students present their information to the class as their classmates take notes. When all reports are done put each city on a card and place them in a box. Students pull a card with a city name and say what they would do in that place. For example: "Si estuviera en Buenos Aires, visitaría __________ y __________ y comería __________." They should be able to complete these statements from their notes.

B. Mapas. Make photocopies of maps of cities from Spanish-speaking countries and give to students. Divide students in pairs and have them give each other directions from one monument or landmark to another. Remind students of phrases used to give directions (**sigue**, **derecho**, etc.).

C. Guided Writing: En Madrid. See p. 287 of the Student Supplement for the drawing and corresponding questions.

D. Entrevistas. Give pairs of students 1-2 minutes to interview each other, then call on several pairs to conduct their interviews for the class.

Partner A - Ask your partner:
- where s/he would like to travel.
- if s/he could help you with Spanish.
- if s/he would go out with someone married.

Partner B - Ask your partner:
- what job s/he would like to have.
- where s/he would go for a honeymoon.
- what s/he would do on a trip to Mexico.

E. Communicative Goals Practice #5. See page 282 of the Student Supplement for the picture and guidelines. For this final oral practice, you may want to challenge students to include other categories of information in their descriptions. For an explanation of how to use these practices as preparation for oral interviews, see p. 16 of the Chapter 2 Teacher's Guide.

F. Round Robin. Divide students into groups of three and put the statements below on an overhead transparency. Students first read the statements as a group. Then Partner A reacts to the statement, Partner B makes a recommendation, and Partner C says what s/he would do in that situation.

MODELO: ¡Miren qué fea que es la foto en mi pasaporte!

A: No creo que sea tan fea en realidad.

B: Te recomiendo que pongas otra foto en tu pasaporte.
C: Si fuera tú, no viajaría y no usaría mi pasaporte.

1. Esteban está perdido en el metro de Madrid.
2. Lourdes necesita encontrar una habitación, pero todos los hoteles están completos.
3. Los padres de Raquel no la van a permitir viajar a México.
4. El guía turístico insiste en que visitemos el Museo de las Momias.
5. Estamos en la playa en Costa Rica, pero no podemos tomar el sol porque hay muchos mosquitos.
6. Juan quiere subir a la boca de un volcán en América Central.
7. Las habitaciones en mi hotel cuestan carísimas -- más de $200.00 por noche.

V. GAMES

A. Travel Jeopardy. Since students have a lot of information from their research on Spanish-speaking countries, this game should work well. You will need to prepare beforehand by writing some questions. Another possibility is to have students write the questions for you, although you will have to edit them before playing the game. To set up the game, put four Spanish-speaking places on the board in a chart like the one below.

ARGENTINA	ESPAÑA	MÉXICO	PUERTO RICO
100	100	100	100
200	200	200	200
300	300	300	300
400	400	400	400
500	500	500	500

Break the class up into teams of 3 or 4 students. Each team will be numbered and will play in turn. Team #1 chooses a country category and a point amount. For example: **"España, 200 puntos."** The questions you ask the team will vary in difficulty depending upon the point amount the team chooses. Here is an example of a series of questions for the "España" category.

100 ¿Cuál es la capital de España?
200 ¿Cuáles son 3 ciudades españolas importantes?
300 Si tu compañero de viaje quiere esquiar en España, ¿adónde le recomiendas que vaya?
400 Nombra 3 pintores españoles
500 Si estuvieras en Madrid, ¿qué museo visitarías?

If Team #1 gets the answers right they get 200 points. If not, Team #2 gets a chance to answer the question for 200 points, and so on. Continue playing until all questions have been asked. You may want to continue the next day with 4 different countries.

B. Verb wheel. You'll need 8 or 9 dice for this game. Give one die to each group of 3 students. The first student rolls the die to determine the person (Wheel 1), the second student rolls for the verb (Wheel 2), and the third rolls for the tense or mood (Wheel 3). Students must write the numbers they rolled and then produce the correct forms.

EXAMPLE: 3 / 2 / 4 Tú no harías nada.

4 / 5 / 5 Ella quiere que nos sentemos.

Students must come up with 10 sentences. The first group to finish wins. While the others are finishing, have the winners put the numbers on the board and their corresponding sentences.

VERB WHEELS

Wheel 1

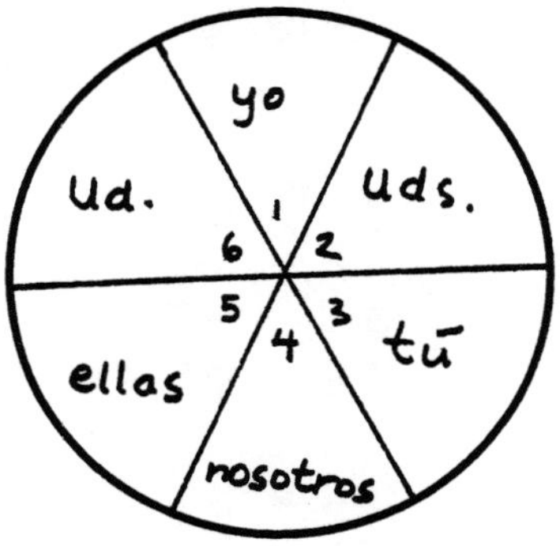

Wheel 2

Wheel 3

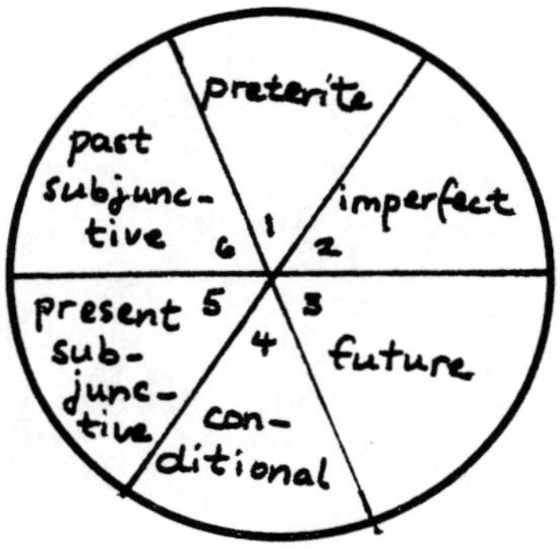

ANSWERS TO SELECTED EXERCISES

ANSWERS TO SELECTED EXERCISES

ANTE TODO

p. 4 Es la una y cuarto de la mañana. Buenas noches. Son las once y cuarto de la mañana. Buenas días. Son las cinco y cuarto de la tarde. Buenas tardes. Son las ocho y cuarto de la noche. Buenas noches.

p. 5 ¿Cuál?, ¿Cómo?, ¿Cuántas?, ¿Quién?, ¿Cómo?, ¿A qué hora?, ¿Qué?/¿Cuántos?, ¿Dónde?, ¿Cuándo?

CAPÍTULO 1

p. 9 1. unos, la 2. los, los, la, la 3. El, el, la, la 4. la, unos, unos, la 5. la, la, el, El 6. unos, los, el 7. el, los, las, la 8. una, la 9. los, la, la 10. El/Un, la 11. los, la, las, la 12. la, unos, unos, una, un, la

p. 10 1. practicamos/estudiamos 2. habla 3. tomas 4. trabaja 5. pagamos 6. desean/toman 7. toca 8. cantamos 9. toma 10. desea 11. compra/necesita 12. compra/necesita 13. pagas 14. hablan 15. trabajan 16. necesita/desea 17. habla/practica 18. regresamos a casa 19. habla 20. desean

p. 11 1. Hay unas palabras nuevas en las pizarras. 2. Nosotros deseamos unas mochilas rojas y unos cuadernos grandes. 3. Las profesoras llegan con unas bolsas y unos libros. 4. En las clases, hay unas ventanas. 5. Mis amigos cantan unas canciones románticas. 6. Los secretarios bolivianos trabajan en unas oficinas pequeñas. 7. Los muchachos descansan porque toman muchas cervezas. 8. Nosotros estudiamos porque deseamos hablar unas lenguas extranjeras. 9. Las estudiantes españolas toman unas clases con los profesores simpáticos. 10. En las residencias universitarias hay unas cafeterías horribles.

p. 12 1. ¿Qué estudias este semestre? 2. ¿Cuántas clases enseña el profesor Dávila? 3. ¿Qué necesitan comprar? 4. ¿Cómo se llama el estudiante extranjero? 5. ¿Cuándo regresa Tomás a la residencia? 6. ¿Por qué estudias el español? 7. ¿Cuánto paga Roberto por los libros de texto? 8. ¿Cómo pagas la matrícula? 9. ¿Dónde trabaja Mercedes? 10. ¿Qué (lengua) hablan Beatriz y Lourdes? 11. ¿Qué compran Uds.? 12. ¿Dónde practican Uds. el español?

p. 13 I. Los artículos: (definido) el, la, el, el, las, las, el (indefinido) un, una, una, unos, unos, un, unas. II. Formas plurales: los actores, las universidades, unas calculadoras, unos problemas, las señoritas, unos dólares, las naciones, los papeles, unas mujeres, unos lápices. III. Pronombres: A. él, ellos, ellas, nosotros B. Ud., tú, tú, Uds.

p. 14 IV. La hora: 1. ¿Qué hora es? 2. ¿A qué hora es la clase de sociología? 3. ¿A qué hora regresas a casa? Expresa en español: 1. Perdón, señorita. ¿Qué hora es? 2. Son las siete en punto. 3. La clase de español es a las once de la mañana, pero la clase de historia es a las cuatro. 4. Necesito estudiar a las tres esta tarde. V. Los números: 1. diez y siete, veintiuna 2. treinta, seis, doce, siete, una 3. veintinueve, veintiún.

p. 15 VI. Gustar: Expresa en español. 9 Me gusta mucho la comida china. 10. Pero no me gustan las hamburguesas. 11. ¿Te gustan tus clases? 12. No me gusta mi clase de física.

p. 16 VIII. Verbos: 1. trabajan 2. deseamos 3. enseña 4. necesitan 5. estudias 6. tomas 7. practico 8. deseas IX. La negación: 1. No, no tomamos cerveza en la clase de español. 2. No, no necesita más dinero. 3. No, no me gusta el coliflor. 4. No, no compran los libros de texto en una biblioteca. 5. No, no hablamos el español perfectamente.

p. 17 X. ¿Qué dices? 1. De dónde eres? 2. ¡Ay, perdón! 3. ¿Te gusta la clase de español? 4. ¿Te gustan los tacos? 5. Mucho gusto. 6. ¿Deseas tomar un café?

CAPÍTULO 2

p. 23 1. Es alemana. Habla alemán. 2. Es del Japón. Habla japonés. 3. Es de Italia. Es italiana. 4. Es de España. Habla español. 5. Es ruso. Habla ruso. 6. Es de Francia. Es francés. 7. Es boliviana. Habla español. 8. Es de Inglaterra. Habla inglés. ¿Cierto o falso? 1. Falso. Es paraguaya. 2. Cierto 3. Falso. Es ecuatoriana. 4. Falso. Son colombianos. 5. Cierto. 6. Cierto. 7. Falso. Son uruguayos. 8. Cierto.

p. 27 Mi vida en la universidad: vivo, se llama, es, toca, habla, creo, debe, viven, asistimos a, comemos, tomo, leo, abre, estudio. Una visita a casa: vivo, vive, regreso, llego, comemos, hablamos, miramos, tomo, hablo, escuchar, bailar, cree, debo, necesito, comprenden, necesito, es.

p. 28 1. Estudio 2. es 3. extranjero 4. colombiana 5. toma 6. hablar 7. tengo 8. las 9. hay 10. llegamos 11. llega 12. se llama 13. tiene 14. Los 15. son 16. un 17. muchos 18. practican 19. trabajan 20. estudiamos 21. gusta 22. cortas 23. practicamos 24. escuchamos 25. deseo 26. necesito 27. tomamos 28. regreso 29. una 30. corta

p. 29 I. B. Definiciones: 1. mi tía 2. mi abuelo 3. mi sobrino 4. mi hermana 5. mi abuelo 6. mis primos II. A. Ser y posesión 1. Es de la abuela. 2. Es del hijo mayor. 3. Son de los padres. 4. Es de los padres.

p. 30 C. Los usos del verbo ser: Soy, Soy, somos, es, es, son. D. La nacionalidad: 1. americano 2. italianas 3. mexicana 4. alemán 5. alemana E. Las preposiciones y los artículos: 1. el, del, de, un, de, la, de 2. La, de la, a, a las, de la. 3. a la, del, los. 4. La, de la, del, La, de los. 5. El, de, del, de 6. El, de, de la, el, de, del. F. Un domingo en casa: 1. llegamos 2. leemos 3. aprende 4. escribe 5. comen 6. miramos 7. regreso.

CAPÍTULO 3

p. 40 ¿De quién son el perro y la chaqueta? Son de la Sra. Ferrer. Son su perro y su chaqueta. ¿De quién son el perfume y la minifalda? Son de Alicia. Son su perfume y su minfalda. ¿De quién son los pantalones negros y los jerseys blancos? Son de las tres muchachas. Son sus pantalones y sus jerseys. ¿De quién son la chaqueta de rayas y la bolsa? Son de la Sra. Guzmán. Son su chaqueta y su bolsa. Los zapatos de tenis son del tío Rafa. Son sus zapatos de tenis. ¿De quién son los aretes grandes y los pantalones azules? Son sus aretes y sus pantalones. La bolsa blanca es de Teresa. Es su bolsa.

p. 41 De compras en el centro: 1. su 2. su 3. su 4. Mi 5. tu 6. sus 7. nuestro 8. su Una familia grande: 1. tu/su 2. mi 3. mis 4. Sus 5. Mi 6. nuestros 7. Mi 8. sus 9. sus 10. mis 11. su 12. su 13. nuestros 14. mis 15. mis 16. sus.

p. 42 La familia: 1. de la 2. de 3. de 4. del 5. del 6. a la, de los, de 7. de 8. al, a las 9. del, de De compras: 1. al, de los 2. de 3. del 4. al 5. a la, a las 6. del, de 7. del

p. 43 Tengo que leer. Quiero leer. Voy a leer. Puedo leer. Tengo ganas de leer. Insisto en leer. Prefiero leer. No tenemos que ir. No necesitamos ir. No vamos a ir. No podemos ir. Marta tiene que regresar. Marta quiere regresar. Marta tiene ganas de regresar. Marta insiste en regresar. Marta puede regresar. Prefieren pagar. Insisten en pagar. Necesitan pagar. Van a pagar. Quieren pagar. Tienen que pagar.

p. 44 1. esta 2. grande 3. los 4. hay 5. mi 6. nuestros 7. vienen 8. asisten 9. es 10. a 11. el 12. del 13. tiene que 14. un 15. desean 16. el 17. contentos 18. creen 19. un 20. puede 21. van 22. prisa 23. quieren 24. Qué 25. desean 26. esta 27. gustan 28. prefiere 29. por 30. latinoamericana 31. primos 32. ganas 33. al 34. voy 35. la 36. rebajas 37. favorito 38. comprar 39. de 40. unos 41. cortos 42. un 43. tengo 44. que 45. el.

p. 46 I. B. En la otra maleta, hay: un traje feo, un traje de baño de lana, unos calcetines morados y verdes, una blusa anaranjada. Pero en mi maleta hay: una camisa de algodón, unas sandalias nuevas, unos pantalones cortos pardos, una camiseta azul. II. A. Los verbos nuevos: 1. vienen 2. quieren, tienen 3. podemos, tienen

p. 47 4. quiere 5. Prefiero 6. tengo 7. prefiere 8. Puede. B. Expresiones con tener: 1. Tengo sueño. 2. Tengo que comprar un regalo. 3. No tiene razón. 4. Tengo prisa. 5. Tengo miedo. C. Los posesivos: 1. tus, tu 2. sus 3. su 4. mi 5. nuestras, mi.

CAPÍTULO 4

p. 55 En la universidad: 1. Entiendes 2. tenemos 3. tienes, leer 4. viene En la residencia 5. Sirven 6. puede, ver 7. vuelve, empieza 8. duermo, hacen. En el centro: 9. almuerzo 10. comprar 11. salgo, vamos 12. haces, quieres La familia: 13. traen 14. pensamos 15. juego, sale 16. ver, pensamos.

p. 56 1. juegan, almuerzan, vuelven, duermen 2. hacen, prefiero, salgo, pedimos 3. salgo, empiezo, pienso 4. jugar, pierde, vuelve, prefiero 5. pide, pierde, duerme, cierra, vuelve, pienso 6. duermo, almuerzo, juego, hago.

p. 57 1. almuerzan, prefiero, sirven, buena, pido, vuelvo, la, empiezo 2. Duermo, duerme, Muchas, está, trabaja, a, Creo, debe, va, vuelve, las, cierra, piensa, tiene 3. Este, quiero, Pienso, vamos, Mis, pensamos, divertido, pierde, del, jugamos, juego, es.

p. 58 1. gustan 2. tengo 3. tengo 4. es 5. estoy 6. puedo 7. duermo 8. tengo 9. hace 10. practicamos 11. hacemos 12. entienden 13. son 14. voy 15.

prefiero Preguntas: 1. Está cansado. Tiene hambre. 2. Practican la gramática. Hacen unos diálogos. 3. No entienden los verbos irregulares. 4. Va a estudiar con una amiga de su clase. 5. Prefiere ir a la cafetería. 6. Porque tiene sueño.

p. 59 A. 1. nos vestimos 2. se bañan 3. me ducho 4. me lavo 5. se acuesta 6. se pone 7. se afeita 8. peinarse 9. nos divertimos B. 1. me despierto 2. me levanto 3. ducharme 4. me visto 5. me pongo 6. Me acuesto 7. me quito 8. me pongo 9. me cepillo 10. me lavo 11. me acuesto 12. me duermo.

p. 61 A. estos, esos; esta, esa; esa; esa, estas; eso B. eso; estos; esos; esa; aquella; estas.

p. 63 II. A. En casa los domingos: 1. duerme, se afeita 2. se despierta, sale 3. Me siento 4. juega, vuelve, se ducha, se pone 5. almorzamos En la residencia: 1. sirven 2. sale, vuelve, pierde 3. nos bañamos, nos duchamos, nos afeitamos 4. duermo, hacen, se acuestan B. 1. esta 2. Eso 3. Ese 4. Esta 5. Esas 6. esta, Eso 7. Eso, Esto

CAPÍTULO 5

p. 74 1. ser 2. ser 3. estar 4. estar 5. estar 6. estar, ser 7. ser 8. ser 9. ser 10. ser 11. ser 12. ser 13. ser 14. ser 15. ser 16. ser 17. estar.

p. 75 1. es 2. están 3. Son 4. están 5. están 6. son 7. son 8. son 9. son 10. están 11. están 12. está 13. estar 14. están 15. está 16. están 17. son 18. está 19. está 20. está 21. es 22. están 23. es 24. es 25. están.

p. 76 1. doctor 2. contento 3. colombiana 4. cansado 5. perezosos 6. preocupada 7. bien 8. cerrada 9. en casa 10. cansados 11. de Panamá 12. de madera 13. sucios 14. cerca de aquí 15. caro.

p. 77 I. Oprah Winfrey es más rica que David Letterman. La Madre Teresa es tan religiosa como el Papa Juan Pablo II. Kramer es más cómico que Fraser. El pelo de Dennis Rodman es menos feo que el pelo de Michael Jackson. Los Smashing Pumpkins son menos populares que los Beatles. Los perros son más cariñosos que los gatos. Brad Pitt es más guapo que Sean Penn. Elizabeth Taylor es mayor que Sharon Stone.

p. 78 A. 1. Nieva. 2. Hace sol/buen tiempo. 3. Está nublado. 4. Llueve. 5. Hace calor. 6. Hay contaminación. 7. Hace buen tiempo/fresco. C. 1. cierto 2. cierto 3. falso 4. cierto 5. falso 6. cierto 7. falso 8. falso

p. 79 A. 1. ser 2. estar 3. ser 4. ser 5. ser 6. estar 7. estar 8. ser 9. ser B. es, Es, estar, es, es, Es, están, ser. C. 1. Gloria tiene tantas clases como Inés. 2. José bebe tantos refrescos como Ramón. 3. Carlos tiene menos amigos que José. 4. Gloria tiene más tarea que Roberto. 5. Luis come más que José. 6. Roberto ve televisión más que Inés. 7. Carlos lee tanto que Gloria. 8. Luis estudia menos que Gloria.

p. 80 D. 1. El bebé está durmiendo. 2. Los niños están jugando. 3. La Sra. Hernández se está bañando. 4. El Sr. Hernández se está afeitando. 5. La abuela se está vistiendo. 6. Susanita se está poniendo el abrigo.

p. 81 F. 1. ¿Dónde está Bogotá? 2. ¿Cuáles son los países centroamericanos? 3. ¿Adónde vas para tus próximas vacaciones? 4. ¿Cuántos habitantes hay en México? 5. ¿De dónde es Carlos Fuentes?

CAPÍTULO 6

p. 88 I.1. saber 2. saber, saber 3. conocer, saber 4. saber 5. conocer, conocer 6. conocer 7. saber 8. conocer, conocer 9. saber 10. conocer II. 1. Conozco, sé 2. saben 3. Sabes 4. sabe 5. saben 6. Sabes 7. conozco 8. Conoces 9. conocer, sé 10. sabes 11. sabe, sabe 12. sé 13. conozco, sé 14. sé

p. 89 1. sabes 2. conozco 3. conozco 4. sabes 5. sabe 6. conocer 7. conoces 8. conozco 9. sabes 10. sé 11. sé 12. conocer

p. 90 La clase: 1. Sí, los conozco bien. (No, no...) 2. Sí, los hacemos. (No, no...) 3. La hago... 4. Sí, lo voy a ver./Sí, voy a verlo (No, no...) 5. La voy a aprender.../Voy a aprenderla... 6. Sí, los empiezo a entender/Sí, empiezo a entenderlos (No, no...) 7. Los compran en la librería. 8. Sí, siempre los ayudo. (No, no...nunca) 9. Sí lo traigo siempre. (No, no...) 10. Sí, es necesario estudiarlas. (No, no...) La comida: 11. Sí, siempre la pago. (No, no...nunca) 12. Sí, a veces lo como antes. (No, nunca...) 13. Lo tomo con azúcar. 14. Sí, me gusta prepararla. (No, no...) 15. Sí, lo traigo. (No, no...) En casa: 16. Sí, siempre los lavo. (No, no...nunca.) 17. Sí la hago todos los días. (No, no...) 18. Lo prefiero poner en.../Prefiero ponerlo en... 19. Sí, las miro. (No, no...) 20. Sí, puedo escucharla.../Sí, la puedo escuchar... (No, no...)

p. 92 1. No hay nada debajo de la cama de Estela. 2. Tampoco hay una pizza en su cama. 3. Ana siempre lleva ropa vieja y sucia. 4. Estela no tiene ningún problema con organizarse. 5. Nadie cree que Ana es una compulsiva. 6. Estela no conoce a nadie interesante. 7. Nadie llama nunca a Estela por teléfono a la una de la mañana. 8. Ana nunca se levanta temprano. 9. No se acuesta temprano tampoco. 10. Siempre llega tarde a clase.

p. 94 Singular: 1. Lea el menú. Léalo. 2. Llama al profesor. Llámalo. 3. No sirva ese vino. No lo sirva. 4. No escriba la carta. No la escriba. 5. Haga/Prepare la cena ahora. Hágala./Prepárela. 6. No abra la puerta. No la abra. 7. Cierre la puerta. Ciérrela. 8. Traiga los bocadillos. Tráigalos 9. Pida los camarones. Pídalos. 10. Pida la cuenta. Pídala. 11. Traiga el helado. Tráigalo. Plural: 1. Esperen a Roberto. Espérenlo. 2. No compren las galletas. No las compren. 3. Estudien el capítulo seis. Estúdienlo. 4. Inviten a Sofía y a Sara. Invítenlas. 5. Hagan el postre. Háganlo. 6. No coman esa tortilla. No la coman.

p. 95 Déla. No la dé. Denla. No la den. Tráigala. No la traiga. Tráiganla. No la traigan. Póngala. No la ponga. Pónganla. No la pongan. Prepárelos. No los prepare. Prepárenlos. No los preparen. Hágalo. No lo haga. Háganlo. No lo hagan. Pídala. No la pida. Pídanla. No la pidan. Llegue temprano. No llegue temprano. Lleguen temprano. No lleguen temprano.

p. 96 Ayúdela. No la ayude. Ayúdenla. No la ayuden. Cómprela. No la compre. Cómprenla. No la compren. Invítelo. No lo invite. Invítenlo. No lo inviten. Úsela. No la use. Úsenla. No la usen. Búsquelos. No los busque. Búsquenlos. No los busquen. Sírvalos. No los sirva. Sírvanlos. No los sirvan. Vaya al café. No vaya al café. Vayan al café. No vayan al café. Páguela. No la pague. Páguenla. No la paguen.

p. 97 II. A. Indefinite and Negative Words: 1. Nunca estudio en la biblioteca porque no me gusta. 2. Ningún compañero estudia allí tampoco. 3. Siempre comemos en la biblioteca. 4. No nos gusta comer nada después de estudiar. 5. No tengo ningún examen esta semana, y mis amigos tampoco. B. Saber vs. conocer: 1. Sabes 2. conozco a, sé 3. conocen a 4. saber 5. conocer a 6. conozco Expresa en español: 1. Sé la respuesta. 2. Vamos a conocer a Juan mañana. 3. ¿Conoces Caracas? 4. No sé cuándo es el examen final. 5. Conoce a muchas personas interesantes.

p. 98 C. (Possible Answers) 1. Los veo... 2. Lo practico con... 3. Los voy a ver/Voy a verlos... 4. Los quiero conocer/Quiero conocerlos... D. 1. ¡No jueguen en el restaurante! 2. ¡Coman toda la comida! 3. ¡Tenga paciencia con los clientes! 4. ¡No haga tantas reservaciones! 5. ¡Pague la cuenta! 6. ¡No salga con Carmen otra vez! 7. ¡No llegue tarde! 8. ¡Vaya en taxi! 9. ¡Traiga más vino! 10. ¡No sea perezoso!

CAPÍTULO 7

p. 108 I. 1. Nos 2. Les 3. nos 4. Te 5. Me 6. les 7. le 8. les 9. nos 10. les 11. te II. 1. me dan 2. le pagamos 3. les mando 4. me compran 5. le piden, les trae 6. le hacen 7. les piden 8. les mandan 9. le dicen 10. me presta.

p. 109 1. le 2. la, la 3. le, le 4. les 5. me, me 6. le 7. lo 8. nos, le 9. me, me 10. los 11. la 12. la 13 La 14. me, le 15. la 16. lo 17. la 18. le, le

p. 111 1. te gustan 2. me interesan 3. les encanta 4. le interesan 5. nos gustan 6. les gusta 7. me encantan 8. les gusta 9. les interesa 10 les gustan.

p. 112 I. 1. El año pasado Fabio viajó mucho. 2. Ayer hice las reservaciones. 3. La semana pasada no escribiste muchas cartas. 4. Anoche comimos bien en el Mesón. 5. Juan llegó de Costa Rica ayer. 6. Anoche hicieron las maletas. 7. El año pasado tomaron el tren a la costa. 8. El año pasado fui agente de viajes. 9. Anoche Uds. trabajaron mucho. 10. Ayer la agencia abrió temprano. 11. El año pasado ofrecimos precios bajos. 12. Anoche volvimos a las once.

p. 113 1. El año pasado saqué muchas fotos. 2. Ayer él buscó el mercado. 3. La semana pasada leímos un libro sobre México. 4. Anoche jugué al vólibol en la playa. 5. Llegué a Madrid anteayer. 6. Ayer María leyó la tarjeta postal. 7. El lunes almorcé en el café de la plaza. 8. El año pasado pagué los boletos con cheque. 9. Comenzaron su viaje la semana pasada. 10. ¿Cuándo volviste del viaje, ayer o anteayer? 11. Ayer se despertaron tarde y perdieron el vuelo. 12. Anoche empecé a hacer la maleta.

p. 115 Catalina Alarcón: 1. Salí 2. fui 3. compré 4. hablé 5. hice 6. pasé 7. regresé 8. entré 9. vi 10. grité

11. llegó 12. me desmayé 13. llamó Jaime Durante: 1. me desperté 2. Me bañé 3. me vestí 4. Tomé 5. salí 6. intenté 7. oí 8. pensé 9. volví 10. llamé 11. llegó 12. Fue 13. explicó 14. perdí. Ramón Torrijo: 1. salí 2. me senté 3. fumé 4. leí 5. sonó 6. tuve 7. pasó 8. contesté 9. Pregunté 10. escuché 11. esperé 12. Fue 13. regresé 14. entró 15. empezó.

p. 117 II. A. 1. le 2. Les, las 3. la 4. me, le 5. le 6. los 7. lo

p. 118 II. B. 1. nos gusta 2. Me gustan 3. les gusta, le gusta 4. me gusta 5. Te gusta. C. 1. No me gusta nada hacer cola. 2. Nos gustaría viajar en primera clase. 3. A muchas personas no les gustan los vuelos largos. 4. No me gustaría ser asistente de vuelo.

CAPÍTULO 8

p. 126 1. Se lo doy. 2. Se lo doy. 3. Me lo da. 4. Te la escribimos. 5. Nos las escribimos. 6. Nos las van a escribir. Van a escribírnoslas 7. Se la quiero dar. Quiero dársela 8. ¿Se la quieres dar? ¿Quieres dársela? 9. ¿Me lo quieres dar? ¿Quieres dármelo 10. Se los vamos a dar. Vamos a dárselos 11. ¿Nos la va a dar? ¿Va a dárnosla? 12. María nos la va a comprar. María va a comprárnosla. 13. Pablo se las compra. 14. Se los compro. 15. ¿Se lo dice? 16. Sus padres se lo mandan.

p. 127 1. ¡Ya se la escribí! 2. ¡Ya se la entregamos! 3. ¡Ya te lo presté! 4. ¡Ya se lo compré! 5. ¡Ya se lo enseñé! 6. ¡Ya te las mostré! 7. ¡Ya se las mandé! 8. ¡Ya te lo di! 9. ¡Ya te los lavé! 10. ¡Ya se la planché!

pp. 128-129 Una cena con amigos. 1. decidió 2. fui 3. volvimos 4. pasó 5. sacudí 6. me bañé 7. se afeitó 8. pusimos 9. llegaron 10. trajeron 11. puse 12. fuimos 13. estuvo 14. preparé 15. serví 16. se quedaron 17. nos divertimos 18. nos reímos 19. dormimos 20. nos levantamos 21. Estuve 22. pude Un aniversario de bodas. 1. hicieron 2. Invitaron 3. preparó 4. sirvió 5. faltó 6. trajeron 7. regalé 8. recibieron 9. leyó 10. se puso 11. se calmó 12. nos divertimos Una fiesta de sorpresa. 1. di 2. fue 3. Quise 4. salió 5. Empecé 6. pedí 7. dijeron 8. se enfermó 9. Volvió 10. se acostó 11. dijo 12. Me puse 13. Pensé 14. tuve 15. Preparé 16. puse 17. serví 18. cerré 19. comencé 20. llegaron 21. vinieron 22. terminamos 23. Fuimos 24. nos sentamos 25. esperamos 26. se despertó 27. Durmió 28. se perdió 29. esperaron 30. dejaron 31. salió 32. vio 33. preguntó.

p. 130 1. durmieron 2. dijo 3. tuve 4. pude 5. vinieron 6. se puso 7. estuvo 8. trajo 9. hubo 10. sirvieron 11. pidió 12. se sintió 13. se divirtieron 14. se despidió 15. se rió 16. sonrió 17. se vistieron 18. pudo.

p. 131 I. 1. Los coches son rápidos, pero los aviones son rapidísimos. 2. Mis otras clases son interesantes, pero la clase de español es interesantísima. 3. Los perros son inteligentes, pero los chimpancés son inteligentísimas. 4. La ciudad de Nueva York es grande, pero el Distrito Federal es grandísimo. 5. Las ratas son feas, pero las cucarachas son feísimas. 6. Los Mercedes son caros, pero los Porsches son carísimos. 7. Jay Leno es cómico, pero Jerry Seinfeld es comiquísimo. 8. Ross Perot es rico, pero Bill Gates es riquísimo. 9. La princesa Carolina de Monaco es elegante, pero la Princesa Diana es elegantísima. 10. Las composiciones son difíciles, pero los exámenes son dificilísimos.

p. 132 I. A. 1. se enojó 2. cumpleaños 3. dar 4. sorpresa 5. entremeses 6. refrescos 7. felicitaciones 8. ponerse II. A. 1 Estos regalos son carísimos. 2. Siempre se siente tristísimo durante la Navidad. 3. Los entremeses son buenísimos.

p. 133 II. B. 1. puse 2. durmieron 3. empiezo 4. sé 5. pudo 6. sirvieron C. 1. puso 2. durmió 3. se despertó 4. se vistió 5. se puso 6. dijo 7. almorzó 8. volvió 9. se sintió 10. estuvo D. 1. ¿Sirvieron entremeses ricos? 2. ¿Vinieron muchos actores famosos? 3. ¿Supiste el teléfono de Sharon Stone?

p. 134 (Section D cont.) 4. ¿Pudiste hablar con Harrison Ford? 5.¿Le trajiste un regalo a Steven? 6. ¿Conseguiste el autógrafo de Andy García? 7. ¿Se divirtieron todos? E. Direct: me, te, lo, la, nos, os, los, las Indirect: me, te, le, nos, os, les. 1. indirect, The indirect pronoun changes to "se." 2. a. Se las voy a comprar. Voy a comprárselas. b. Mis padres me las mandaron ayer. c. Te lo voy a contar. Voy a contártelo d. Se las necesito dar. Necesito dárselas. e. Ella nos lo está explicando ahora. Ella está explicándonoslo. F. 1. Me lo compraron. 2. Se las mandé 3. Se la mandamos. 4. (Ella) se los está sirviendo ahora. Está sirviéndoselos ahora.

CAPÍTULO 9

p. 143 A. 1. era 2. vivía 3. iba 4. hablaba 5. ayudaban 6. comíamos 7. jugábamos 8. tenía 9.

volvíamos. B. 1. tenía 2. trabajaba 3. iba 4. salíamos 5. volvíamos 6. pasábamos 7. Nos divertíamos C. apagaba, dormía, desayunaba, salía, llegaba, escuchaba, hacía, tenía.

p. 146 I. 1. Cuántos 2. Por qué 3. Qué 4. quién 5. Qué 6. Cuál 7. Adónde 8. Cuál II. 1. Qué 2. cuál 3. cuáles 4. Qué 5. Qué 6. Qué 7. Qué 8. qué

p. 147 I. C. pasatiempos, actividades, ir al cine, deportes, ciclismo, fútbol, béisbol, partidos, equipos, juega, aficionados, gana.

p. 148 II. A. 1. Tomás escribía una carta. 2. Nuria y Benito comían una hamburguesa. 3. El Sr. Cárdenas leía una revista. 4. Teresa y Roberto miraban la televisión. 5. La Sra. Cárdenas leía una novela.

p. 149 II. D. 1. ¿Qué vas a hacer este fin de semana? 2. ¿Cómo se llama el grupo que va a tocar? 3.¿Qué tipo de música tocan? 4. ¿Dónde van a tocar? 5. ¿Cuánto cuestan las entradas? 6. ¿Cómo se llama su nuevo disco?

CAPÍTULO 10

p. 156 1. Eran, empezó 2. era 3. Conoció 4. llamó 5. servía, sonó 6. Se sentía 7. Tenía 8. Trajo 9. Quería 10. lloraba, hablaba 11. Tomó 12. Estaba

p. 157 1. Eran 2. empezó 3. se levantó 4. llamó 5. puso 6. estaba 7. tenía 8. Tomó 9. Estaba 10. era 11. entró 12. estaba 13. sacó 14. Estaba

p. 158 (Possible answers): 1. Cuando llegó al consultorio Juanito estaba un poco nervioso. No le gustaba ir al médico. 2. Su mamá habló con la enfermera. Le dijo que su hijo se sentía mal. 3. Mientras la enfermera escribía, su mamá esperaba. La enfermera era muy amable. 4. Luego el médico lo examinó. Juanito ya no tenía tanto miedo. 5. Después, la enfermera le dio una medicina. Aunque no quería, Juanito la tomó. 6. Cuando salió estaba contento. Ya se sentía mejor.

p. 161 1. que, que, quien 2. que, lo que, que 3. que, quien, Lo que 4. quien, que, quienes 5. quienes, que, quien 6. que, Lo que 7. quien, quienes, que 8. que, Lo que, que 9. lo que, quien, Lo que.

p. 162 1. se conocían 2. se vieron 3. se hablaron 4. Se dijeron 5. se querían 6. se dieron la mano 7. se odiaban 8. se encontraron 9. se besaron 10. se escribieron 11. verse 12. se abrazaban 13.. Se dijeron 14. se querían 15. se prometieron

p. 163 II. A. 1. llegaron 2. pidió 3. tenía 4. trajo 5. sabía 6. conocía 7. recomendó 8. decidió 9. pidió 10. esperaron 11. había 12. estaba 13. iban 14. quería 15. llegó

p. 164 II. A. 16. era 17. acabaron 18. preguntó 19. quería 20. dijo 21. prefería 22. Pagaron 23. caminaron 24. daban 25. gustó 26. tenía 27. pensó 28. eran 29. dijo 30. iba 31. dijo 32. era 33. tenía 34. era 35. volvió 36. pasó Preguntas: 1. Una cerveza, porque tenía mucha sed. 2. Porque había mucha gente en el restaurante. 3. Quería tomar un helado. 4. Estaba cerca del restaurante, pues caminaron allí. 5. A Raquel le gustó, pero Paco dijo que era una película tonta. 6. Pasó toda la noche con las luces encendidas. B. 1. se conocieron 2. se casaron

p. 165 (Section B continued) 3. se vieron 4. miraron 5. se hablaron 6. hablándose 7. abrazándose 8. besándose 9. Se quieren 10. casarse C. 1. que 2. Lo que 3. que 4. que 5. que 6. que 7. quienes

CAPÍTULO 11

p. 171 (Possible answers): I. Hace veinte años que soy estudiante. Hace diez y nueve años que sé leer. Hace tres años que estudio español. Hace dos años que vivo en esta ciudad. Hace veinte años que conozco a mi mejor amigo. Hace dos años que practico mi deporte favorito. II. Hace un mes que vi a mis padres. Hace tres semanas que tuve una cita. Hace un año que fui a la playa. Hace un mes que hice un viaje. Hace seis meses que di una fiesta. Hace seis semanas que estuve enfermo.

p. 172 1. A Ana se le rompieron los platos. 2. Se les perdieron las llaves. 3. A Bill se le acabó el dinero. 4. Se nos olvidaron los pasaportes. 5. A Marta se le cayeron los huevos. 6. A José siempre se le olvida mi nombre. 7. A Sara y Laura se les quedó el perro en casa. 8. A Yolanda se le olvidó mi teléfono. 9. Se nos quedaron las entradas en casa. 10. Se les acabó el champán.

p. 173 A. 1. Se le acabó 2. se me cayó 3. se nos quedaron 4. se te rompieron 5. se les perdieron B. 1. Se le perdió la cartera. 2. Porque se le acabó el dinero. 3. Porque se nos olvidó. 4. Porque se le rompieron los platos y vasos. 5. Porque se le cayeron al suelo. 6. Porque se me quedó la llave en el coche.

7. Se le rompió una pierna. 8. Se le olvidaron los libros. 9. Porque se me olvidó comprarla.

p. 174 (Possible answers) Se le rompió el brazo. Se le acabó el dinero. Le duele el estómago. Se acuerda de su cita en el Restaurante Casa de Eva. Se le olvidó la hora de salida de su vuelo.

p. 175 1. por, para 2. por 3. Para, por 4. para 5. para, para 6. para, por 7. Por, para 8. por, para 9. Para 10. para 11. para, por 12. por, para 13. para 14. por 15. para

p. 176 1. para 2. por 3. por 4. por 5. Para 6. por 7. para 8. por, por 9. para 10. para, por 11. para 12. por 13. por 14. por, para 15. Para 16. Para 17. por 18. por 19. Para 20. Para

p. 177 B. 1. Se hizo daño en el pie. 2. Se cayó por la escalera. 3. Sufrió muchas presiones. 4. Se dio con la puerta.

p. 178 A. 1. Hace ocho años que Isabel toca la guitarra. 2. Hace dos años que Isabel tiene los gatos. 3. Hace una hora que los gatos están en el sofá. 4. Hace treinta segundos que suena el teléfono. B. 1. Hace quince minutos que puso el estéreo. 2. Hace un mes que compró el sofá. 3. Hace dos meses que volvió a la universidad. 4. Hace treinta minutos que empezó a leer. C. 1. se les olvidaron 2. se le perdió 3. se me quedan 4. se nos acaba 5. se me cayó

p. 179 E. 1. constantemente 2. pacientemente 3. rápidamente 4. tranquilamente 5. puntualmente

p. 180 F. 1. para, por, por, para, por 2. Por, para, Por, por, para, por

CAPÍTULO 12

p. 186 1. No, no está bien. No la uses. 2. Sí, está bien. Sácame una. 3. Sí, está bien. Ponlo. 4. No, no está bien. No lo grabes. 5. Sí está bien. Límpialo 6. No, no está bien. No los saques. 7. No, no está bien. No la manejes. 8. Sí, está bien. Siéntate. 9. Sí, está bien. Tócalos. 10. No, no está bien. No lo lleves. 11. Sí, está bien. Escúchalos. 12. Sí, está bien. Léelo. 13. No, no está bien. No lo lees. 14. No, no está bien. No lo cambies. 15. Sí, está bien. Míralos 16. No, no está bien. No lo lleves.

p. 189 I. 1. lea, nos dé, vaya, nos explique 2. hablemos, estudiemos, practiquemos, vengamos, durmamos 3. vayas, visites, comas, hagas, lleves 4. saque, salga, busque, encuentre II. (Possible answers) 1. ...no me llame a la una de la mañana. 2. ...estudiemos por lo menos un poco todos los días. 3. ...me regalen un Porsche. 4. ...coma menos hamburguesas. 5. ...pague la mitad de la matrícula. 6. ...me presten cien dólares.

p. 190 1. Quiero que salgas. Sal. No salgas. 2. Recomiendo que comas allí. Come allí. No comas allí. 3. Recomiendo que lo hagas. Hazlo. No lo hagas. 4. Deseo que no vayas hoy. Ve hoy. No vayas hoy. 5. Quiero que lo compres. Cómpralo. No lo compres. 6. Me alegro que busques trabajo. Busca trabajo. No busques trabajo. 7. Es importante que pidas un aumento. Pide uno. No pidas uno. 8. No quiero que veas esa película. Vela. No la veas. 9. Necesito que me traigas el libro. Tráemela. No me la traigas. 10. Prefiero que no lo pongas allí. Ponlo allí. No lo pongas allí.

p. 191 (Possible answers) 1. Le recomiendo que cambie su vida. 2. Le recomiendo que busque otro trabajo. 3. Le recomiendo que siempre limpie bien la cocina. 4. Le recomiendo que se case. 5. Le recomiendo que les dé pruebas con mucha frecuencia. 6. Le recomiendo que duerma una siesta por la tarde. 7. Le recomiendo que haga ejercicio. 8. Le recomiendo que salga de la universidad. 9. Le recomiendo que trabaje menos y salga más con los amigos.

p. 192 2. Vuelvo a casa. Quieren que yo vuelva a casa. 3. Él fue al partido. Quiero que él vaya al partido. 4. Uds. cantan. Uds. cantaron. 5. Hacen la tarea. Quiero que ellos hagan la tarea. 6. Lo explicamos. Quiere que nosotros lo expliquemos. 7. Pago la cuenta. Quieren que yo pague la cuenta. 8. ¿Ayudaste en casa? Recomendamos que tú ayudes en casa. 9. Salgo el lunes. Salí el lunes. 10. ¿Hiciste la tarea? Te recomiendan que hagas la tarea. 11. Leen el libro. Quiero que Uds. lean el libro. 12. Llegan temprano. Llegaron temprano. 13. Buscó su tarea. Recomienda que él busque su tarea. 14. Cambian el canal. Quiero que Uds. cambien el canal. 15. Manejan en la lluvia. Manejaron en la lluvia. 16. Compro otro acuario. No quiere que compre otro acuario. 17. Arreglaron todo. Recomiendo que arreglen todo. 18. Uds. esperan. Uds. esperaron.

p. 193 I. C. 1. el correo electrónico 2. el alquiler 3. el/la jefe/a 4. la camioneta 5. la bicicleta 6. el pez 7. el televisor 8. el equipo fotográfico 9. el ratón 10. falla

p. 194 II. B. W will/wish (querer, desear) E emotion (alegrarse, sentir) I impersonal expressions (es necesario, es importante) R requests (ordenar, permitir) D doubt/denial (dudar, no creer) O ojalá II. C. pueda, comprenda, comience, pague, haga, llegue, tenga, escriba, viva, dé, esté, venga, hable, sea, piense, vaya, practique, diga

p. 195 D. (Possible answers) 1. ...estudiemos mucho 2. ...no nos dé tantas pruebas. 3. ...le preste cien dólares. 4. ...no me pida más dinero. 5. ...acabe pronto mis estudios. 6. ...me deje en paz. E. 1. regrese, vivir 2. hablen 3. busquen, ganar, puedan 4. está 5. salga 6. tengamos 7. vaya F. 1. Quiero que abras el libro. Ábrelo. 2. No quiero que leas el periódico en clase. No lo leas. 3. Quiero que estudie esa página. Estúdiela ahora. 4. ¿Las respuestas? Quiero que las escriban. Escríbanlas, por favor. 5. ¿El vocabulario? Les recomiendo que Uds. lo estudien. Estúdienlo esta noche.

CAPÍTULO 13

p. 205 1. se levante 2. practique 3. dé 4. aprendamos 5. tienen 6. prepare 7. pasen 8. vaya 9. visite 10. quieren 11. hagan 12. llame 13. invite, compre 14. espere 15. es 16. haga

p. 206 1. te cases 2. seas 3. estés 4. quiero 5. tengo 6. digas 7. sepa 8. eres, pasemos 9. es, te olvides, busques 10. puedo 11. estés 12. pienses, nos separemos 13. es, seamos, vas 14. voy

p. 207 1. estudie... 2. apenden... 3. tenga... 4. es... 5. da... 6. hagan... 7. es... 8. haga... 9. sea... 10. baile... 11. vayan... 12. llegue... 13. esté... 14. cante... 15. esté... 16. sea... 17. ayuden... 18. sea...

p. 208 (Possible answers) 1. No me gusta que... 2. Creo que... 3. Dudo que... 4. Pienso que... 5. Es verdad que... 6. No creo que... 7. Es verdad que... 8. Recomiendo que... 9. Dudo que... 10. Temo que... 11. Espero que... 12. Ojalá que... 13. Creo que... 14. Ojalá que... 15. Es verdad que...

p. 209 1. a 2. a 3. que 4. de 5. de 6. X 7. a 8. X 9. de 10. X

p. 210 I. A. ruinas, arquitectura 2. artesanías, cerámica, tejidos 3. ópera, compositor, cantantes 4. obras, pintores, pintura. II. A. W will/wish (querer, desear) E emotion (alregrarse, sentir) I impersonal expression (es necesario, es importante) R requests (ordenar, permitir) D doubt/denial (dudar, no creer) O ojalá

p. 211 II. B. 1. S 2. I 3. S 4. I 5. I 6. S 7. S 8. S 9. S 10. I 11. I 12. S C. 1. haya 2. vaya 3. puede 4. vuelva 5. va

CAPÍTULO 14

p. 219 1. puesta 2. hechos 3. escrito 4. rota 5. lavada, planchada 6. apagado 7. hechas 8. guardados 9. cerradas 10. organizado 11. ha mandado 12. haya(n) subido 13. haya pedido 14. haya resuelto 15. hayan venido. 16. hayan estudiado 17. ha explicado 18. hayan hecho 19. ha leído 20. han sacado

p. 220 I. 1. hayan vivido 2. construida 3. pintada 4. han decorado 5. cuidado 6. hayan puesto 7. he tenido II. 1. haya corregido 2. ha dicho 3. organizado 4. haya sacado 5. memorizados 6. ha puesto 7. haya escrito 8. preparado 9. hayamos ido

p. 221 I.1. haya escrito 2. hemos estado 3. se ha muerto 4. se haya mejorado 5. Han llegado 6. ha dicho 7. han empezado 8. hemos cambiado 9. ha estado 10. haya contestado II. 1. Porque se ha muerto su suegra. 2. Han llegado dos chicas americana. 3. Una es muy buena y come de todo. La otra es un problema. 4. Han comenzado la escuela. 5. Ha visitado Elizabeth. Es de Cádiz.

p. 222 I. A. naturaleza, ritmo de vida, soledad, madruga, monta a caballo, construir, proteger, destruir C. 1. el aceite, la gasolina 2. llantas 3. parar 4. el taller 5. el/la conductor/a 6. gastan 7. frenos

p. 223 II. A. visto, pedido, vuelto, puesto, descubierto, abierto, ido, dicho, muerto, invitado, hecho, visitado, roto, escrito B. 1. un río contaminado 2. un bosque protegido papel reciclado 4. un parabrisas roto 5. un problema resuelto 6. un coche estacionado C. 1. ¿Sara ha encontrado trabajo? 2.¿Lucho ha salido con muchas chicas? 3.¿La universidad ha mandado mis notas? 4.¿Mi novia se ha quedado en casa? 5.¿Mis amigos me han escrito muchas cartas? 6.¿Lola ha tenido otro accidente de coche? 7.¿Has alquilado mi cuarto a alguien? 8.¿Jaime ha cuidado a mi gato?

CAPÍTULO 15

p. 230 1. sea, me ayude, pague, cocine, vea 2. sea, tenga, ande 3. esté, sea, cueste, tenga 4. haya, sea, pueda 5. sea, sepa, llegue 6. sean, empiecen, den, expliquen 7. respete, escuche, haga, gane, trabaje

p. 232 1. Sí, hay dos hombres que juegan al ajedrez. 2. No, no hay nadie que lea el periódico. 3. Sí, hay gente que come en el café "Alemán" 4. No, no hay nadie que juegue al fútbol. 5. No, no hay nadie que saque fotos. 6. Sí, hay varias personas que dan un paseo. 7. Sí, hay alguien que toca la guitarra. 8. Sí, hay alguien que pasea en bicicleta. 9. Sí, hay alguien que espera a un amigo. 10. Sí, hay varias personas que discuten.

p. 233 1. cante, escriba, traiga, hace, es 2. haya, van 3. sepa, quiere 4. hable, tenga, pueda, pide 5. sea, cuesta, hay, buscan

p. 234 (Possible answers) 1. Yoli tiene tiempo de limpiar la casa, a menos que los invitados lleguen temprano. 2. Yoli piensa comprar hielo extra en caso de que a Jorge se le olvide. 3. Virginia va a la fiesta con tal que no vaya Luisa. 4. Los amigas de Yoli van a comprar la comida hoy para que ella pueda preparar los entremeses esta noche. 5. Jorge va a trae su estéreo para que puedan escuchar música en la fiesta. 6. Yoli va a hacer la fiesta en el patio a menos que llueva. 7. Yoli debe estar en casa antes de que lleguen unos amigos para ayudar. 8. Yoli va a llamar a todos los amigos para que sepan a qué hora empieza la fiesta. 9. Yoli puede ir al supermercado en caso de que se le olvide a Carmen comprar las bebidas. 10. A menos que la fiesta termine a la una, los vecinos van a llamar a la policía.

p. 235 1. Mercedes y Gloria van a jugar al tenis con tal que haga buen tiempo. 2. Antes de que vaya al partido de béisbol el Sr. Martínez va a lavar el coche. 3. La Sra. García empieza a preparar la cena a las siete para que la familia pueda comer a las ocho. 4. Claudio va a ir a la discoteca a menos que tenga que trabajar. 5. Antes de que mire la televisión Marta tiene que estudiar dos horas. 6. En caso de que no llame Miguel, Ana va a salir con Alberto. 7. María va a la piscina con tal que haga mucho calor. 8. Antes de que duerma la siesta Lorena tiene limpiar la casa.

p. 237 1. tenga 2. sea 3. acaba 4. he 5. quieras 6. veamos 7. eres 8. seas 9. veamos 10. guste 11. decides 12. dé 13. hayas 14. veamos 15. empieza 16. llegue 17. ir 18. perder 19. esté

p. 238 I. A. 1. divorciarse 2. pareja 3. la vejez 4. la amistad 5. la luna de miel 6. separarse B. 1. el nacimiento 2. la infancia 3. la niñez 4. la adolescencia 5. la vejez 6. la muerte II. A. 1. N/I 2. N/I 3. N/I 4. E/D 5. E/D 6. N/I 7. E/D 8. E/D 9. E/D

p. 239 B. Antes de que Para que A menos que Con tal de que En caso de que C. 1. lleves 2. cuides 3. te olvides 4. saques 5. entren 6. pueda 7. tengas 8. eres 9. pase 10. llamas 11. estemos 12. se diviertan

CAPÍTULO 16

p. 245 1. Voy al banco. Fui al banco. Iba al banco. Iré al banco. Quiero que vayas al banco. Ve al banco. 2. Busca trabajo. Buscó trabajo. Buscaba trabajo. Buscará trabajo. Sus padres quieren que busque trabajo. Busca trabajo. 3. Salgo de la oficina a las cinco. Salí a las cinco. Salía a las cinco. Saldré a las cinco. El jefe no quiere que yo salga a las cinco. No salga a las cinco. 4. Pago las facturas. Pagué las facturas. Pagaba las facturas. Pagaré las facturas. Quiero que mi compañero pague las facturas. Paguen las facturas. 5. Quiero ahorrar dinero. Quise ahorrar dinero. Quería ahorrar dinero. Ahorraré dinero. Mis padres quieren que ahorre dinero. Ahorra dinero.

p. 246 1. se divorciarán, se casará, estará, intentará 2. se pondrá, empezarán, veremos, se reunirán, harán 3. se casarán, trabajarán, recibirá, ganará, tendrá, se caerá, romperá

p. 248 I. Future, Past, Habitual, Future, Future, Habitual, Habitual II. Subjuntive, Indicative, Indicative, Subjuntive, Subjuntive, Indicative, Indicative III. 1. necesitaba 2. pagaban 3. pagó 4. recibe 5. compra 6. pueda 7. den

p. 249 1. estudia 2. llame 3. vieron 4. tiene 5. entraron 6. lleguen 7. estén 8. salen 9. terminen 10. tienen 11. regresó 12. haya 13. den 14. acabe

p. 250 1. Cuando sea grande, Carlota será ama de casa y tendrá dos hijos. 2. Cuando Federico sea grande será un científico muy famoso. 3. Cuando Ricardo sea grande jugará fútbol americano profesional. 4. Cuando sea grande, Luis trabajará para una empresa grande y ganará mucho dinero. 5. Cuando sea grande, Daniela se casará con un hombre muy guapo y rico. 6. Cuando Sergio sea grande, será un futbolista muy famoso. 7. Cuando sea grande, Sonia será una juez de la Corte Suprema. 8. Cuando sea grande, Antonio será programador de computadoras. 9. Cuando sea grande, Pedro será arquitecto. 10. Cuando sea grande, Amalia será doctora.

p. 251 I. B. 1. préstamo, cobrar 2. al contado 3. sucursales 4. presupuesto 5. cuenta de ahorros 6. ahorrar, gastos

p. 252 1. Trabajan tres cajeros en el Banco Central. 2. Tendrá poco dinero. 3. El Sr. Ruiz cobra un cheque. 4. Lo cobrará para comprarle un regalo a su esposa. 5. Tendrá una cuenta corriente. 6. Pide un préstamo porque necesita dinero para pagar la factura de su tarjeta de crédito.

p. 253 1. iré 2. estudiaré 3. conoceré 4. invitará 5. nos casaremos 6. será 7. abriremos 8. Tendremos 9. estaremos 10. Tendremos 11. Viviremos 12. iremos

p. 254 1. Indicative. Cuando Fred da una fiesta, siempre invita a mucha gente. 2. Subjunctive. No podemos irnos hasta que yo encuentre mis llaves. 3. Subjunctive. Cuando llegue Enrique, quiero hablar con él. 4. Subjunctive. Se les va a acabar la comida antes de que nos vayamos. 5. Subjunctive. Le ayudaré a Fred a hacer la limpieza, después de que termine la fiesta. 6. Indicative. Lo pasamos bien, hasta que llamaron la policía. 7. Indicative. Después de que se fue Paco, Laura bailó con otro.

CAPÍTULO 17

p. 261 1. llegaron, llegaran 2. mandaron, mandaran 3. ayudaron, ayudara 4. eran, fuera 5. dieron, dieran 6. hicieron, hiciera 7. dijeron, dijera 8. decidieron, decidieran 9. compraron, compráramos 10. invitaron, invitara

p. 262 1. acompañara 2. me pusiera 3. hablara 4. viniera 5. me sentara 6. llamara 7. supiera 8. pasara 9. volviera 10. se casara 11. hiciera, pudiéramos 12. trajeran 13. vinieran 14. nos calláramos 15. se rompieran

p. 264 1. Pues, el nuestro es magnífico y grandísimo también. 2. Pues, los míos son muy amables y divertidos también. 3. Pues, el mío trabaja en Alemania y el Japón y es ejecutivo para un banco internacional. 4. Pues, el mío también tiene un jardín grandísimo, y tiene un hombre que lo cuida. 5. Pues, el mío es programador de computadoras y tiene su propia compañía. 6. Pues, la mía está casada con el embajador de Francia. 7. Pues, la mía es perfectísima.

p. 265 1. tuya 2. mía 3. suya 4. suya 5. suyos 6. nuestros 7. suyos 8. suyos 9. suyos 10. tuyas 11. mías 12. suyas 13. tuyas 14. suyas 15. mías 16. tuyo 17. suyas 18. mía 19. tuyas 20. míos 21. mía

p. 266 I. B. 1. un asesinato 2. el testigo 3. gobernar 4. una guerra 5. el noticiero 6. una huelga 7. la ley 8. un desastre

p. 267 II. A. 1. salieran 2. comieran 3. fuera 4. existieran 5. viniera 6. pasáramos 7. apagaran 8. pudiera 9. durmiera 10. tuviera B. 1. Era importante que todos votaran. 2. Lo malo era que no había ningún candidato capaz de gobernar. 3. No creía que los políticos tomaran en serio sus deberes. 4. Leíamos varios periódicos todos los días para que estuviéramos enterados. 5. Y mi padre insistía en que viéramos el noticiero todas las noches. 6. Era horrible que la prensa tuviera más interés en desastres que en la política.

p. 268 C. 1. fui 2. tomamos 3. tardó 4. Fue 5. decidimos 6. quería 7. pintara 8. fuera 9. pudiera 10. Tuve 11. terminó 12. vi 13. gustó 14. salió 15. parecía 16. tuviera Preguntas: 1. Viven en Sevilla 2. Porque Concha quería que un artista pintara su retrato. 3. Para que su novio pudiera ponerlo en la mesita al lado de su cama. 4. Por que la nariz salio demasiado grande, y el cuello parecía como el de una jirafa.

p. 269 E. 1. mía, tuya 2. mío 3. nuestro 4. suyo 5. suyas

CAPÍTULO 18

p. 272 Los sueños de Teresa y Juan: 1. gustaría 2. sería 3. podríamos 4. pintaríamos 5. Tendría 6. podrías 7. aprendería 8. compraríamos 9. andaríamos 10. Estaríamos El viaje espacial de Rafael: 1. encantaría 2. iría 3. visitaría 4. conocería 5. explicaría 6. Se casaría 7. construiría 8. empezarían 9. llegarían 10. tendría 11. Preferiría 12. extrañaría 13. podríamos

p. 274 (Possible answers) 1. A Celia le gustaría ir a Europa. 2. No tiene mucho dinero, así que haría un viaje económico. 3. Se quedaría en pensiones baratas. 4. Viajaría por autobús y por tren en segunda clase. 5. Tendría que ahorrar mucho para poder hacer el viaje. 6. Gonzalo tiene mucho dinero, así que viajaría en primera clase. 7. Iría a hoteles de lujo. 8. Le gustaría hacer un viaje por mar. 9. Alquilaría un coche y viajaría por toda Europa. 10. Pagaría todo con tarjeta de crédito.

p. 275 (Possible answers) 1. Si yo ganara la lotería, haría un viaje por todo el mundo. 2. Si tuviera más tiempo, aprendería a tocar la guitarra. 3. Yo iría de viaje si tuviera más dinero. 4. Si no fuera estudiante, trabajaría para una empresa grande. 5. Mis padres estarían más contentos conmigo si yo los visitara con más frecuencia. 6. Si pudiera hablar con el presidente, le diría que no me gusta su política. 7. Si no tuviera la clase de español, iría a ver una película. 8. Estaría más feliz si no tuviera tanto que hacer. 9. El mundo sería mejor si yo fuera presidente. 10. Si estuviera de vacaciones estaría más tranquilo. 11. Mis amigos y yo daríamos una fiesta enorme si tuviéramos más tiempo y dinero. 12. Si pudiera conocer a cualquier persona, conocería a Gong Li. 13. Si tuviera una cita con Brad Pitt no hablaría de sus películas estúpidas. 14. Mi vida sería menos complicada si no fuera a la universidad.

p. 278 II. A. 1. iría 2. haría 3. viajaría 4. querría 5. saldríamos 6. visitaría 7. podríamos

p. 279 (Section A continued) 8. tendríamos 9. querrías B. (Possible answers) 1. Si yo estuviera en Cancún, México, iría a ver las ruinas en Chichén Itzá. 2. Si yo pudiera viajar a cualquier país, iría a Chile. 3. Si yo visitara las ruinas de Machu-Picchu, llevaría un abrigo conmigo porque hace frío allí. 4. Si mis amigos y yo hiciéramos un viaje a España, nos quedaríamos una semana en Sevilla. 5. Si yo fuera a la Ciudad de México, iría al Museo de Antropología. C. 1. tendría 2. correría 3. tuviera 4. viajara 5. iría 6. llegara

p. 280 Querido Profesor/a ___, Tenía Ud. razón, Sevilla es increíble. Llegué la semana pasada y ahora me estoy quedando en una pensión barata. Los dueños son tan amables y la comida es excelente. Esta ciudad es tan diferente y encantadora. Me encanta que la gente sea tan amable y que yo practique el español. Nos vemos el semestre que viene.